Patterns in Design, Art and Architecture

Petra Schmidt, Annette Tietenberg, Ralf Wollheim (eds.)

Edition form
Birkhäuser – Publishers for Architecture
Basel · Boston · Berlin

Contents

Annette Tietenberg
The Pattern Which Connects

Without doubt: patterns are an issue in design, art and architecture just now. Crockery is striped; gumboots are spotted; sofas floral. In fashion circles deliberate harking back to the fabrics of the 1970s seems de rigeur, and firms which produce patterned wallpapers to suit their clients' wishes and offer one-off items instead of woodfibre paper are enjoying increasing demand. Artists are discovering the principle of allover again, whilst renowned New York galleries do not hesitate, after years of abstinence, to show the early work of a pioneer of op art like Victor Vasarely. And after all, in the realm of architecture, we are coming across ornamentation and patterns all over the place: on exterior facades, in interiors, even as a constructional principle.

A revival of patterns would, all the same, not rate a mention – and certainly not an opulent book of patterns from A to Z – if it were simply a question of one of the many ephemeral trends, which will soon have passed its peak and then be levelling off. But people who value only the brief optical attraction in patterns and anticipate from a system of décor nothing more than a colourful rejuvenation of their own living-space, they are missing the point. As history teaches us, for more than a hundred years the question of décor, at least from a eurocentric viewpoint, has always come paired with the question of morality.[1]

Even someone who has never read the polemical piece "Ornament and Crime"[2], which Adolf Loos published in a progressive lower case typeface in 1909, can depend on the fact that their own notions of "good" and "bad" taste are still arguably influenced by those distinctions, which Loos initiated at the beginning of the twentieth century. Adolf Loos' condemnation of décor has impressed itself deeply on cultural memory, according to which the "evolution of culture is synonymous with the removal of ornamentation from utility objects", as the architect, sated with the ostentation of Viennese art nouveau, put it. As a committed representative of his profession, Loos criticises particularly what he sees as the superfluous cloaking of facades, the feigning of neo-classical and neo-baroque elements. He deems the state-subsidised "plague of ornamentation" an ominous step backwards for the whole of humanity. And he locates the need to decorate walls, skin and useful objects on the lowest level of cultural development: he does actually countenance cavemen, who carved magic signs into stone, a child at play and the non-European, uncivilised peoples, like the Papuans, decorating their surroundings and their bodies. If the bourgeois succumbs to the "drive to

ornamentation", then they publically confirm that they are not in a position to restrain themselves.[3] They cannot control their instincts and put themselves in that way on a level with a criminal, who is not prepared to subordinate his individual needs to the rules of society. His asocial attitude can be recognised not least by the way he covers his body with tattoos.[4] Ornamentation that decorates the human body and buildings, as well as utility objects, is then, according to Loos, a dependable index for criminal energy, childish behaviour, sexual recklessness and dissipated hedonism – with other words: a sure sign of the degeneration of society.

The unusual severity with which Loos passes judgement on ornamentation can only be understood if you consider his sign argumentation in its historical context.[5] On the one hand, Loos, who had spent three years in the United States after studying architecture in Dresden, had come into contact with the puritan work ethic and had subsequently been a convinced advocate of Louis Henry Sullivan's motto: "form follows function". On the other, he had to witness, on returning to Europe at the turn of the century, the "decline of craftsmanship"[6] and an unprecedented inflation in ornamentation. What craftsmen had earlier produced laboriously, retaining century-old traditions, machines could now produce quick as the wind in any desired quantity and in almost any materials: frills, tendrils intertwining and floral features. The Berlin architect Hermann Muthesius duly asserted: "Yes, mass industrial production took on the externals of craft aspirations on a false basis and in that way produced merely all the more falsely because it began to use machines to imitate forms, which previously had belonged only to manual production and had originated from its nature. You need only point to the supply of the art-industrial market with that cheap mass bric a brac, like embossed tin ornaments, machine-produced carving, moulded leather decoration and whatever all the surrogates and imitations of the last art-industrial period are called."[7] Around 1900, the utility objects, which are turned out inexpensively as mass-produced goods, had surrogates for craft manufactures in the form of traditional motifs applied to them, to ensure a favourable response from a substantial public. Critics like Muthesius and Loos sensed deceit in this "machine-made ornamentation". Here a little wrap of lies was being draped, so they suspected, around an object, which was designed and produced in a division of labour typical of the industrial society. The traditional floral motifs, the tendrils, roses and lilies, with which the goods were decorated, obstructed honest and practical dealing with the new forms of production.[8] For, according to Loos and Muthesius, on the basis of their function buildings and objects proper to the times would not have needed all this effort. They, therefore, judged the holding onto the habitual systems of ornamentation, which was supposed to give mass-produced goods a stamp of individuality, as a sign of reactionary ways of thinking and nostalgic exaltation.

Ornamentation lends itself particularly well to this sort of argumentation precisely because it differs by definition from patterns by being described as an additive element, something attached subsequently. Otherwise patterns and ornamentation have more similarities than differences. Both rest on the principle of repetition and both present a perfectly proportioned relation between patterns and background. And with motifs, they are governed by the same repertoire: they employ floral forms, bands of clouds and fabulous beings like dragons or phoenixes, comprehensible symbols, then, for fertility, divine or mythical powers. Or they stick to formalised basic schemes like uninterrupted and broken symmetries, which correspond to nature's blueprints or mathematical operations. The decisive difference is, however: ornamentation is applied to a functional basic form, whilst patterns are an integral element of the load-bearing construction. Two examples demonstrate this difference best: facade cladding, the function of which consists in making the construction beneath it invisible, and a coat tailored from a woven material. The coat and patterns are inextricably connected with each other; they are one. The facade elements, by contrast, can take on any desired appearance and, should whoever commissioned the building not like them any more, they can also be replaced with alternative designs.[9] As something added on afterwards, ornamentation easily falls under the suspicion of being superfluous junk. And so Loos undergirds his plea for the banning of ornamentation for ever from High Culture, above all with economic considerations. It would be straightout waste, squandering of capital, labour, material and time, to carry on producing ornamented objects. He promises paradisical conditions to all those who were not grieving for the formal repertoire of the past, but had recognised the trend of the times and were ready to abandon unnecessary embellishments. Alongside the added value aesthetically, the case would have a decisive economic value too: workers, who would not have to torment themselves with imitating what was once the beautiful would then only need to work four hours a day in future, would consequently be able, however, to enjoy higher wages as they would be producing higher-value goods.

In this way, Adolf Loos utterly underestimated the inherent dynamic of automation and capitalism. It certainly did not occur to him that the production of low-value objects was already being promoted by the state around 1900 because people anticipated commercially a much greater benefit from the consumption of ephemeral trash dependent on fashion trends than from the establishment of an efficient production and distribution system for high-value manufactures. Although he lacked economic farsightedness, Loos became one of the most important heralds of modernity with his polemic "Ornament and Crime" because he eloquently advocated a new aesthetic in production. Whatever was no longer produced by human hands but by machines had to, according to his thinking, have a corresponding look too: neat, smooth and tidy. Significantly, it was producers like architects and designers, who picked up this thesis, carried it forward and made it, for instance, into the guideline for the Weimar and Dessau Bauhaus. The cherished habits of users, who had gladly clung to the time-honoured formal repertoire, were a thorn in his side. Certain of their aesthetic and moral superiority, progressive architects and designers refused outright to make any concessions to "uncultivated" investors and consumers. At the same time, they saw themselves duty-bound to develop a programme of aesthetic education, which was meant to raise those whom they saw still dwelling on a level with children, savages and criminals to the status of cultivated people. Consumers, according to the subtext of modernity, had to learn to see with the eyes of the producers. And they had to be trained up to renouncing voluntarily and joyfully everything that was not absolutely necessary.

But seeing with the eyes of the producers also meant for the consumers discovering a new sort of beauty, a beauty which owes its existence to the absence of what is superfluous and a concentration on what is absolutely necessary. In other words: buyers and users of utility goods, although they were situated at the other end of the production chain, gradually came to like seeing and thinking like designers and entrepreneurs. They began to scorn signs of excess and opulence, which had previously seemed desirable to them as guarantees of wealth and power, like a cardinal sin and to surround themselves with formal expressions of efficiency. In this way, modernity made its entry into living rooms not only as an aesthetic but also as an economic principle: the reduction to essentials.

The formal expression of efficiency was, in design as in architecture, long synonymous with the absence of ornamentation and patterns.[10] Acceptable were only a few tidy structures and smooth, monochrome surfaces, which seemed best suited to the mechanical production of utility objects. As consumers adopted the perspective from the aesthetics of production, that led, as Pierre Bourdieu could demonstrate in his investigation "Distinction. A Social Critique of the Judgement of Taste"[11], gradually to the establishing of a new class system, one which was not dependent on background and family ties, but on level of education. Since the 1920s according to Bourdieu, an ostensibly ascetic lifestyle could for decades signal belonging to the educated upper class, whilst fondness for decorations became the characteristic trait of vulgarity. Whoever was planning to go up in the world would buy Mies van der Rohe's Barcelona Chair; whoever wanted to demonstrate belonging to the Ruhrpott coalfields stayed with the baroque style of furniture jokingly named after the mining town of Gelsenkirchen.

This restrictive model first began to crack in the wake of pop trends and the flower-power movement. With the psychedelic patterns, which made their entry into living rooms and wardrobes in the 1970s, a suspicion started to grow that a human was indeed certainly more than a rational being. Everything that Adolf Loos considered the black pits of the soul, the opponents of rationality and functionality, now "blossomed": the ecstatic, the sensory gratification, the erotic. As part of a youth and protest culture patterns seemed then once more – to stay with the Freudian model where Adolf Loos had sought counsel – to be allied with the id. Patterns remained a symbol of the wild instincts; they still stood for the uncivilised, the unrestrained and the sensuous. They were set, more or less deliberately, against the uniformly grey world of the bourgeois, against the functionalism of the Establishment.

It was not until postmodernity that breaking up the structure of social distinctions and traditional building forms and decorative systems could be made presentable again with any success. In the form of over-sized columns, artificial furs and patterned lamination the decade-long repressed ornamentation and patterns returned to the home pastures. And with them long unacknowledged emotions. Albeit at the price of drowning everything, which once had meant tradition and significance, in irony. The columns were too big, the décor too gaudy, you could only admit to yearning for your old home with a spiteful laugh, a mildly hysterical laugh, which had inscribed into it the knowledge of an irretrievable loss.

Since the turn of the century it has seemed possible for the first time to bring in that reconciliation of practicality and ornamentation, from which Ernst Bloch once vouchsafed the generation of your hometown.[12] For it has been obvious for a few years now that designers have been orientating themselves quite unconstrainedly and naturally to the often contradictory needs of consumers. The dominance of production aesthetics would seem to be finally over, and more than ever designers allow the useful objects they create not only a function but also an emotional component and a communicative potential. So they pay hommage to that décor once demoted to the status of the superfluous as they take the excess of nature as their model and cover lamps, tables, chairs or vases with depictions of leaves, blossoms or animals. Contrary to the designers of the 1980s, who were steeped in the theories of postmodernity and

avoided nature-motifs and launched free patterns as irritants into the functionality-worshipping world of utility objects, today's acolytes of the floral pattern eschew demonstrative ironical ruptures. They cotton, rathermore, deliberately onto patterns rich in tradition and onto old craft techniques – like Paul Simmons, a member of "Timorous Beasties" from Glasgow, who has looked at the landscape motifs in the country's typical blue and white colours, as we know them from old tiles, and has combined them with fragments from contemporary life, like airplanes and cars, or the Rotterdam designers Jurgen Bey and Hella Jongerius as well, who work in the context of the loose cooperative "Droog". Their message runs: you must not break with the past completely in order to arrive in the present. So, when she got the opportunity of working together with the deeply traditional porcelain manufacturer Nymphenburg, Hella Jongerius readily recalled how valuable crockery once functioned: at the courts of kings and princes, plates and tureens had to have more to offer than just holding food. They were supposed to serve display purposes and, as "Conversation Pieces", keep the talk flowing around the table. Jongerius's designs continue the thread, which was laid down in the past; albeit that the designer reserves the freedom not only to apply hunting trophies to the plates: in this place of honour she also makes room for a rhino, no less, which she bedecks moreover with a floral patterned stole. Patterning is here not only an eye-catcher but also part of a narrative arrangement: it invites you to elaborate on an amusing story.

Décor lends objects local colour and identity – that is something designers and consumers have equally come to value in the meantime. For just because they are linked to the past, décors do not have to be, as Adolf Loos once declared, obsolete both anachronistically and in production techniques. For example, Tord Boontje, born in the Netherlands town of Enschede in 1968, also works on a historical idiom of imagery with innovative production methods. Before he went to France, he had been living in London since 1991 and studied at the Royal College, which is why the British have accepted him – despite his unmistakable accent – as one of their own: in 2003, the British Council declared him Designer of the Year. Boontje identifies with his elective homeland by reaching back to pattern books from the Victorian age. But unlike William Morris, from whose wallpaper, carpet and fabric patterns he likes to draw inspiration, Boontje does not dream of a revival of medieaval craft techniques. Where Morris held industrial production responsible for the ugliness of the cities, Boontje does not see any conflict between stylised forms of nature and mechanical production. Quite the contrary: it is only the application of innovative technologies that has enabled him to produce, for example, the lamp, Wednesday Light, which has a steel flower garland winding around a naked light bulb, for a wide range of consumers. Since a high-tech precision cutter has been employed, the vegetable forms can also be teased out of the brass without any problems. Accordingly the production costs could be reduced, and the lamp is scarcely more expensive than a bunch of flowers.

While Adolf Loos, with a social-reformist impetus, once located the better world in a distant future, in which décor had retreated before a pure functionalism, Tord Boontje puts his faith completely in the present and he stages paradise very concretely and colourfully with the help of the company Moroso: under his direction interiors become jungles, in which lianas dangle from the ceiling and luxuriant foliage covers armchairs and chairs. So profligate Nature, applied formulaically, seems to regain those cultural spaces, which humans once wrenched from it when they began to erect walls and build houses.

Yet it is in this case a tamed Nature, from which no danger emanates any more and on whose terrain dark nature-spirits no longer practise their mischief. For Nature seems to us today – just think of the use of genetic engineering – to be a construct through and through. And so it is no longer considered, as has been the case since antiquity, the antithesis to technology, but itself as a technical invention. If people once worshipped it as the all-creative principle, which art and culture were to imitate, so it has itself meanwhile come to obey the economic principle of absolute efficiency and has to submit to the logic of a simple reckoning of cost and use value. In its constructedness it can be recognised particularly clearly in the floral pattern, which owes its effect from way back to its formulaic nature, to its level of abstraction and its disembodiment.

Beyond that, floral patterns fulfill ideally all demands of production in series: as an anonymous creation they are reproducible without copyright fees. Their motifs can be repeated as often as desired, in every required size and can be represented in the course of various production processes. And in addition, they count as popular and comprehensible across all language barriers, but are all the same excellently suited to link into local traditions. Décor is today far more than superfluous knick-knackery or pointless waste, then: it shows the current state of technology, which determines our existence, and it allows us to anchor ourselves in our history. To that extent, it is only logical, if today it is no longer the cold, predictable calculation of the Protestant work ethic that has become the guiding principle for design, but the teeming, freely extendable expansion of patterns. Conforming to the premises of a consumer society, which does not define itself through self-denial but through hedonism, efficiency-become-form has retreated before

excess-become-form. Things look quite different in the area of art. Adolf Loos did admit that the rules he promulgated could only claim validity for architecture and design but not for art. For, at the beginning of the 20th century, the fronts had long been staked out: design was considered a hotly disputed field. Here it was a question of themes relevant to social politics, like the use of things, the organisation of work-sharing processes, the social and aesthetic results of industrialisation, innovative production techniques, the use of new materials and commercial thinking. Fine art could, by contrast, be regarded as detached from such profane questions, yet the price was being marked out as the "Other". Art became a reserve for everything that no longer had a place in an industrialised society: self-determination, non-alienated work, mastery in handiwork, mythical thinking, self-reflection and the subjective view on the world. Art, belonging to a higher sphere and simultaneously regarded suspiciously for its uselessness, Loos equated in its function with ornamentation. He declared verbatim: "I can tolerate the ornamentation of the Kaffir, of the Persian, of the Slovakian peasant woman, the ornamentation of my cobbler, for they have no other means to reach the high points of their existences. We have art, which has replaced ornamenation. After the burdens and toils of the day, we move on to Beethoven and to Tristan. My cobbler cannot do that. I may not take his pleasures away from him, as I have nothing else to put in their place (...) the humans of the common herd have to differentiate themselves through various colours; the modern human needs his clothing as a mask. His individuality is so enormously strong that it cannot express itself in items of clothing any more."[13]

Adolf Loos is once again speaking here about social distinctions. "Simple people" like farmers and cobblers may carry on enjoying childish spectacles like ornamentation and patterns, so his argumentation goes. The upper class, by contrast, would not need such trivia, for it knew the incomparable joys of sublimation: it knew how to enjoy art. From Loos's viewpoint, art and ornamentation hence serve the same purpose, even if they direct themselves at different circles: they allow people to enjoy themselves and their environment as aesthetic constructions, as inventions. Art and ornamentation are, accordingly, both visible signs of individuality, and the singularity of the self shines through all the more brightly, the more the world of utility goods acknowledges, by contrast, the uniformity of mechanical aesthetics.

Art in the 20th century was, therefore, never affected by the verdict against patterns and ornamentation to the same extent as architecture or design. Nevertheless, it could not risk intruding into the realm of the useful and concrete; their task remained the reflection of perception, their particular territory the space of illusion. So a close convergence between science and art, between mathematical processes and the use of patterns in painting can be observed in modernity. This development experienced its high point at the end of the 1940s, when Max Bill, co-founder of concrete art, analysed "The Mathematical Approach in Contemporary Art"[14] through debating with Max Bense's writings on information aesthetics. Bill regarded it as his task to assist art to establish the elements of and to perfect an organisational system, which was based on mathematical rules. Bill believed in the construction of a "pure gaze". As logic seemed to him to be the sole guarantee of truth, he assembled his compositions only out of basic geometrical forms.[15] In his painting he was concerned with creating schemata, operations of symmetry, redundancy and variety. Whilst the representatives of concrete art in patterns were looking, then, for immutable codes, the "flicker boys", who were subsumed under the concept "op art" by an unknown author in "Time",[16] showed themselves truly fascinated by the fact that human perception is anything but dependable. Following Victor Vasarely's experiments, artists, who had formed the Groupe de Recherche d'Art Visuel (GRAV), as well as individualists like Almir Mavignier, Michael Kidner and Richard Anuskiewicz, set about painting patterns, which were so confusing and complex that they overloaded the capacity of the human eye to discern an object. To this end, they relied on effects like after image, moiré and transforming figures. In the 1960s the name op art became a notable label, the suggestive effect of which even a singular painter like Bridget Riley never could quite evade, although she repeatedly distanced herself from this stylistic concept: "I have never studied optics and my use of mathematics is rudimentary and confined to such things as equalizing, halving, quartering and simple progressions. My work has developed on the basis of empirical analyses and syntheses, and I have always believed that perception is the medium through which states of being are directly experienced. (Everyone knows, by now, that neuro-physiological and psychological responses are inseparable)."[17] Her participation in the exhibition, "The Responsive Eye", which took place in 1965 at the Museum of Modern Art in New York, brought her much praise and recognition. On the other hand, she was disconcerted by the unexpected success: she had become a star overnight. Her visual motifs were copied and came to be used as window decoration in fashion shops. Her black and white patterns had become independent, and in the process the significant debates on the problem of figure and ground in painting fell by the wayside.

Bridget Riley's shifting between the dissolution and the genesis, her patient sounding out of pictorial levels, which she achieves with dazzling colour contrasts, loose strewing of dots or meandering formations of stripes, so-called "colour twists", is still today trailblazing for a younger generation of artists, which has committed itself to All-over and is pursuing the potential of colour and the dynamics of the pictorial space in depth. And Jochen Twelker reinforces the plastic effect emanating from patterns of stripes still further by choosing opening motifs like shirts, pullovers or blouses, which are worn on the human body. The closeness to fashion, which irritated Bridget Riley so much that she (unsuccessfully) undertook the attempt to protect her painting from the infringements of the commercial world by legal methods, is something artists like Bettina Allamoda and Vanessa Beecroft consciously create, when they concern themselves with the way patterns work. Just as designers are no longer satisfied with creating useful things, so artists no longer allow themselves to be limited solely to the reflection of painting's methods, to engendering metaphorical models and sensitive inwardness. They deal self-consciously with the fact that what they develop in their pictures mostly gains recognition in reproductions. Peter Zimmermann hence makes a point out of the technical bases of the media images by enlarging the networks of dots, which we can scarcely recognise with the naked eye vis-à-vis reproductions, and making them into the sole pictorial motif. And Susanne Paesler concerns herself with the gesture of repeat painting, with the "effect of simulating visuality by depending on the media, to make a picture on a textureless painting surface look as if it were painted on a photographic screen"[18], as Hanne Loreck writes. Others, like Elke Haarer and Parastou Forouhar, use the digital possibilities of copying[19] to highlight the aggressive effect behind the familiarity of motifs, which comes with well-known patterns, by minimal modifications. Then again, Yayoi Kusama, Michael Lin and Peter Kogler push on into concrete spaces, cover walls, floor and ceiling with patterns. And in addition, Peter Kogler even manages the trick of carry on writing, with the help of a gigantic screen, the evolutionary history of the braided band – as far as the streak pattern, which the art historian Alois Riegl had begun to note in 1893.

Patterns are above all one thing: border-crossing. They are equally at home, in biology and information science as in philosophy and behavioural science, in the past as much as in the present. So whoever works with patterns is close to no longer knowing any limits. To describe the relationships between corresponding parts, the deeper symmetries, which are concealed by asymmetries on the surface, the theorist of evolution, Gregory Bateson, once talked about "the pattern which connects". He writes: "What pattern connects the crab to the lobster and the orchid to the primrose and all the four of them to me? And me to you? And all the six of us to the amoeba in one direction and to the backward schizophrenic in another?"[20]

Such a basic pattern, that forms a link between unequal parts despite all obvious differences, also seems to connect art and design with each other. What was once united and was violently separated more than one hundred and fifty years ago, could – a hope motivated by the contemporary developments – shift back closer again: namely, fine and applied art.

1   cf. Hal Foster, Design and Crime (and other Diatribes) (London/New York: 2002).

2   This text is based on a talk with which Loos shocked the Viennese public in 1908: Adolf Loos, Ornament and Crime, Lecture 1908, in: Adolf Loos, Ornament and Crime. Selected Essays. (Studies in Austrian Literature, Culture, and Thought Translation Series: 1997).

3   Self-restraint has masculine connotations for Loos, the feminine he locates on the level of the subconscious, the instinctive and the erotic.

4   Tattooing counted since the middle of the 19th century up to the 1980's as an anti-bourgeois sign. The tattoo customary in the South Seas was imported by seamen into Europe in 1774 following Thomas Cook's expeditions. There tattoos were initially feared due to their magic effects and their proximity to "uncivilised savages", but were also admired because they identified their bearer as a person who had seen the "earthly paradise" with their own eyes. In the 1870's, investigations in criminological anthropology began, which were intended, on a so-called scientific – and with that 'objective' basis – to demonstrate a causal connection between bodily and moral defects. As many tattoos were found in workhouses, hospitals and prisons, doctors like Cesare Lombroso came to the retrospective conclusion that tattoos were a sign of criminality. Their thesis found wide assent, because the "sign on the skin" already carried historically negative connotations: tattoos seemed a logical continuation of the mediaeval practise of branding and tattooing as a form of punishment. See: Stephan Oettermann, Zeichen auf der Haut. Die Geschichte der Tätowierung in Europa [The Sign on the Skin. The History of Tatooing in Europe] (Frankfurt/Main: 1985).

5   Loos wrote his talk in an intellectual climate, in which for the first time there was talk of sublimation of the instincts and the overcoming of the infantile spiritual life and hallucinatory regressions. In this context, one has to note that Sigmund Freud's "The Interpretation of Dreams" had appeared in Vienna in 1900 and his "Three Essays on the Theory of Sexuality" in 1905. Otto Weininger's "Sex and Character" was published in 1903. Loos's vocabulary demonstrates that he had concerned himself with psychoanalytical writings.
See Ronnie M. Peplow, "Adolf Loos: Die Verwerfung des wilden Ornaments [The Rejection of the Wild Ornament]", in: Ornament und Geschichte. Studien zum Strukturwandel des Ornaments in der Moderne, ed. Ursula Franke/Heinz Paetzold (Bonn: 1996), pp. 173–189.

6   Ernst Bloch, "Bildung, Ingenieurform, Ornament [Education, Engineering Form, Ornament]", in: Eckhardt Siepmann, Kunst und Alltag um 1900. Jahrbuch des Werkbund-Archivs (Gießen: 1978), p. 387.

7   Hermann Muthesius, "Redebeitrag auf der Verhandlung des deutschen Werkbundes zu München am 11. und 12. Juli 1908 [Contribution to the debate of the German Werkbund in Munich on the 11th and 12th of July 1908]", in: Die Veredelung der gewerblichen Arbeit im Zusammenwirken von Kunst, Industrie und Handwerk (Leipzig: 1908), pp. 37–53, here p. 40.

8   On the reception of the critique of ornamentation, see also María Ocón-Fernández, Ornament und Moderne. Theoriebildung und Ornamentdebatte im deutschen Architekturdiskurs (1850–1939) [Ornament and Modernity. The formation of theory and the debate on the ornament in the German discourse on Architecture (1850–1939)] (Berlin: 2004).

9   Like every scheme, this one also has its snags. It is, for instance, difficult in the case of applied patterns, which are affixed subsequently to an object, a plate or a cup, for instance. And also the coat already mentioned can be produced, without more ado, by using various materials, without having to change the cut.

10   In this context, the demand for serving your material surfaces. The designer gets the job of allowing the genuine qualities of a material to show up clearly, instead of transforming, or even concealing them.

11   Pierre Bourdieu, La distinction (Paris: 1979).

12   Ernst Bloch, Geist der Utopie. 1. ed., facsimile of the edition of 1918, (Frankfurt/Main: 1985): p. 48 (The Spirit of Utopia (Stanford: 2000)).

13   Adolf Loos, "Ornament und Verbrechen (1908) [Ornament and Crime]", in: Adolf Loos, Trotzdem. Gesammelte Schriften 1900–1930, ed. Adolf Opel, (Wien: 1982), pp. 77–88, here p. 88.

14   Published in: Pevsner, Vantongerloo, Bill, Ausstellungskatalog Kunsthaus Zürich [Exhibition Catalogue], (Zürich: 1949), no page.

15   In a sort of inversion of the argument, mathematicians, who concerned themselves with Benoît Mandelbrot's algorhythmic representations of fractal geometry, fancied themselves as artists. Hence the German Mathematical Society plumed itself in 1990 for its centenary with images on the topic of "Seeing Mathematics". And in the Museum of Modern Art, photographs from the realm of chip architecture were shown alongside constructivist art on the occasion of the exhibition "Information Art".

16   Anonymous, "Op art: Pictures that attack the eye", in: Time, vol. 84, no. 7 (London: 23rd Oct. 1964).

17   Bridget Riley, "Perception is The Medium", Art News, (New York: Oct. 1965).

18   Hanne Loreck, "Medialer Realismus [Mediumistic Realism]", in: Susanne Paesler, ed. Berlinische Galerie (Berlin: 2005) pp. 21–24, here p. 22.

19   See Peter Phillips/Gillian Bunce, Repeat Patterns. A manual for Designers, Artists and Architects (London: 1993).

20   Gregory Bateson, Mind and Nature: A Necessary Unity (New York/Dutton: 1979), p.8.

Ralf Wollheim
On the Construction of Surfaces – Patterns in Architecture

"Look, the time is nigh, fulfillment awaits us. Soon the streets of the town will glisten like white walls. Like Zion, the holy city, the metropolis of heaven. Then we shall have fulfillment."[1]

It is scarcely a hundred years ago that Adolf Loos was predicting those white cities. In a pointed and extremely influential polemic he condemned everything that was decorative in architecture, arts and crafts. And for generations to come it almost seemed he had been proven right. With the Werkbund, the Bauhaus and the International Style, ornaments and sumptuous décors did indeed disappear. Modernist architects and their successors designed plain, simple structures with a strong emphasis on construction and on purity of material. But all over the world structures have recently arisen, in which décor and colour, images and patterns have been used. In this way, department stores and luxury boutiques have acquired eye-catching facades and interiors. The exteriors of the buildings are meant to match the glamour of the goods. A wedding chapel shaped like a clam, complete with starry skies, is, however, for some still something romantic, but for others the threshold into kitsch has already been passed. The public likes it. Of course, it likes to be surprised and enjoys the new opulence. In a media-dominated society, architecture also has to assert itself visually in the big city jungle.[2] Those sorts of attention-grabber belong to the investor's "Brand Mission", whether it is high tech for Adidas or glamour for Gucci. But the architectural quality of the buildings bears no direct relation to the "show effect" of their intended impact. Contrary to the widespread suspicion of everything decorative, a conspicuous facade or an unusual pattern does not exclude good architecture. In professional circles it is above all more subtle projects that are being extensively discussed. There too, it is a question of rediscovering images, ornamentation and patterns. The attendant intellectual debate refers, however, to the architectural relationship of exterior or facade to the structural unit, to construction and décor, as well as to the historical ban on ornamentation.

Patterns and surfaces
First of all, three examples are to be more closely examined as representing the elementary patterns in architecture. Forms of décor arose from relatively simple structures and conventional elements. Through nothing more than a mild degree of alienation, everyday surfaces become patterns. The architects Baumschlager and Eberle chose a massive parquet in Canadian maple for the foyer of a Munich insurance company. The richly contrastive parquet, made out of brown, beige and reddish spars, is here, however, continued across the walls and the ceiling. Thus, the foyer appears to be a closed box, in which top and bottom are treated equally. Through the parallel laying, there arises, according to viewpoint, dynamic-looking perspectives or the calmer impressions of a horizontally arranged pattern. Nägeli Architects used a similar alienation effect for their single-family houses in Berlin, which duly got the nickname parquet buildings. Here, wood was not only employed for construction, but also for the exterior cladding. Their fishbone pattern made of larch timber, borrowed from the interior, stresses the verticality of the tower-like living blocks standing amid lofty fir trees. At the same time, the unusual diagonal pattern creates a varied play of colour and light as well as a surprising spatial effect. Daniele Marques is, in the final analysis, relying likewise on the strategy of alienation. With the structure for a community centre, which comprises administration, fire brigade and workshops, he has chosen an extremely irregular planking for the exterior walls. Rough planks of varying width generate a strong relief in the black-stained concrete. Compared with the standard exposed concrete walls from the 1970s, the pattern derived from the production process seems graphically enlarged and unusually plastic. For all that, this disturbing of the usual proportions, this shift in proportion, is only the result of a particular selection from building materials. The patterns of these three projects were derived from the sort of technical details one can find in almost every structure. Only the alienated application of the materials and the irritating proportions make patterns from the relatively banal elements.[3] Architects developed these astonishing patterns through variations in quite simple means of construction. As the structure of the walls corresponds with their patterns – there is a unity of structure and décor – it is difficult to talk about superfluous ornamentation here. Many new patterns in architecture are structurally necessary details and hence scarcely consistent with the category of applied ornament.

Pattern and ornament
In general, we differentiate between the concepts of ornament, ornamentation and decoration. Ornament, as embellishment, as adornment, as the individual motif respectively, is defined in contrast to ornamentation as the sum of an ornamental vocabulary from an epoch or a style. The ornament is not by its nature an independent entity, but needs a vehicle. Many contemporary buildings stretch the concept of ornamentation to the limit, for the vehicle of the pattern and the pattern itself can scarcely be distinguished from each other. The character of something applied is just not there or can only be demonstrated with difficulty. Where the construction stops and the decoration begins depends, then, on whether an interpretation is strict or benevolent. In the extremely reduced formal language of

contemporary building, architectural element and pattern can only be separated by interpretation. There exist, at best, rudimentary ornaments, which could be more precisely described as patterns. Two examples, where the pattern conforms to the construction, can make this clear.

Pattern and construction

This is how the glass facade designed by Herzog and de Meuron for the shop of Prada in Tokyo works firstly as an exterior, which consolidates the building with its variously raked roof planes and sets it apart as a notable stand-alone unit from its heterogeneous surroundings. Various rhombic elements made of glass – planar, concave and convex – underline the crystalline character of the building. The irregular pattern of facets on the facades frames what is going on inside to produce quasi-cinematic images. But the expressive, rhombic steel structure girding the building is at the same time a part of the supporting structure as well. The Office for Metropolitan Architecture tackled a library in Seattle in quite another way. Here are various suspended – rather than loadbearing – facades with a rhombic pattern, which are assigned to different areas in the building. The built facade with glass fronts variously raked according to the need for daylight, and the urban structural context matches the collage of partially staggered stacked zones. The repeated piercing of the facade acquires a dynamic intensification by the rhombic bracing, which emphasises the shift in inclination with great effect. Whilst with the typical screening facades of modernity a static lattice exposes the physical and constructional circumstances, the logic of construction is here, in the truest sense of the word, inverted. The effect of the facets in the facade reinforces the collage-like character of the library and emphasises how the previous organisation of things has been abolished. An extreme example of the unity of construction and pattern is found in a residence in Japan by the Atelier Tekuto. From outside, the chequerboard pattern of the facades appears truly conventional. But inside, the system of single rectangular elements, stacked one on the other like bricks, reveals itself. "Cell brick" is what the architect Yamashita calls his design. For the single steel boxes coated in ceramics were welded into larger units for the exterior walls and then screwed together. Here, it is the pure construction that forms and determines the outward appearance. Such design elements do not lend themselves to being subsumed under the concept of ornamentation any longer. It is not a question of individual forms of adornment but of the repetition of technical details, which determine the construction of the facades and the interior spaces of the buildings. The elements used are integral constituents of the design as well as the construction; they were not added on subsequently and they can, therefore, not be removed without substantial losses. In this way, the contemporary patterns stand in a modernist tradition, which is characterised by reduction of the means employed and by typification and seriality. And they were developed from the same logic of construction.

Patterns and images

The use of graphic surfaces, or, respectively, the use of images for facades stands for the new application of patterns. The library of the university in Eberswalde is an extreme example of patterns in architecture, which employs images much more intensively than other buildings already cited. And its relation to the art history of the last decades is much more pronounced. By contrast, the residence in Aggstal stands for an application of a very reduced craft pattern, which explores the relationship of construction to graphic surface. When the library was presented to the public in 1999 by Herzog and de Meuron, there was widespread astonishment. The facade of the severely cubic building is composed of images. Only on closer inspection does it become clear that the rows of images are not added on as a second layer, as an exterior. The concrete, the structure itself is the vehicle for the images. The motifs from art history as well as the historical photography of political and private events, all chosen by the artist Thomas Ruff, reveal themselves as relief-like depressions in the concrete or as screenprints onto a few glass elements.[4] Depending on how the light falls, the impression of a strongly structured surface shifts to that of a seemingly closed, smooth-sided box. Minimal art and pop art, Donald Judd and Andy Warhol are the contrary godfathers of this design, which combines an extreme plastic reductionism with a plethora of images. Architecturally, it unites a rigorously rational construction with the ornamentation once believed lost, or rather with patterns.[5] By contrast, the Studio Hild and K uses quite conventional masonry for a residence in Aggstal. In its rural surroundings, the family house with its gable roof does not stand out initially. Yet viewed from closer up, the roof turns out to be unsymmetrically shortened on one side, and the facade reveals a brickwork and whitewash diamond-pattern décor. The geometrical pattern does not end exactly at the corners, but is extended around the building's edges. On a graphic level, the relief made out of tiles seems very much like a textile cladding, without any direct relationship to the construction. At the same time, the massive relief emphasises, however, the traditional, solid masonry structure. This paradoxical phenomenon is further intensified by the disarticulated geometry. For the regular sequence of the diagonals has, in side view, no relation to the pitch of the roof. Here the rhombic pattern coalesces, as it does at the frames of the windows and the doors, into a hugely projected edge. Both projects show a treatment of patterns, which is closely linked to construction. At the same time the architects work with breaches in the decorative system – here in the shift from concrete to glass as well as with a rhombic pattern which does not close off – and in that way make the surface décor of the buildings into a theme. What is characteristic, also for the other buildings in this book, is, however, the serial repetition of the motifs. As with the repeat patterning of wallpaper, the basic elements could be continued across an area at will. That is why the concept of pattern is more appropriate than that of ornament for considering contemporary architecture. The buildings of Sauerbruch Hutton Architects also work with a graphic quality in facades. With their GSW highrise in Berlin, they use the vertical sunscreen slats between a double-skinned glass facade to transpose a complex – and mutable – colour rhythm onto a gigantic surface. They used a similarly irregular pattern made of colour areas with the help of coloured interior mounted blinds at the phototechnics centre in Berlin-Adlershof. In later projects, they then varied the principle of the "allover-pattern", with irregularly distributed, coloured facade elements. The exterior of the buildings becomes an image, which can assert itself in the context of urban building. Here, too, it is a case of patterns rather than ornamentation.

Ornamentation and modernity

In his lecture, "Ornament and Crime"[6], Adolf Loos sermonised on unadorned surfaces, straight lines and right-angled edges. Almost a hundred years ago, he damned not only art nouveau, with its luxurious formal language, but also everything decorative. And he prophecied a future, which would completely renounce embellishment, patterns and ornamentation. For, according to Loos, only primitive cultures would cover all objects with patterns. All this culminated in the comparison with tattooing, which only criminals or perhaps degenerate aristocrats sported.[7] He identified cultural progress with an increasing renunciation of decoration. At the latest with art nouveau, craft and the longtime lowly category of ornamentation acquired a dominant position. Designing uniformly in a style with curving lines and floral ornamentation dominated graphics, design and painting. And with historicism, architecture also entered a border zone between the free and the applied arts.[8] It only re-established itself as an art of engineering construction in the 20th century. Construction and rational design suited the economic and industrial conditions of the time. Accordingly, Le Corbusier set out his understanding of progress leading to rational form: "From the primitiveness of the Early Christian Chapel, we pass to Notre Dame of Paris, the Invalides, the Place de la Concorde. Feeling has been clarified and refined, mere decoration set aside and proportion and scale attained, an advance has been made; we have passed from the elementary satisfactions (decoration) to the higher satisfactions (mathematics)."[9] The emphasis on rationality, on

creating forms through technology and construction, did not, however, lead to architecture being regarded as a purely utilitarian art. Abstraction as the epitome of modern building was transformed from the supra-individual, anonymous qualities of technology and carried over into the area of aesthetics, of art.[10] With that came the separation of ornamentation and architecture. Although both are purposive, ornamentation was associated with craft skills and assigned to the lower arts. The rationalisation of building through standardisation, typification or modularisation was promoted at the Bauhaus particularly by Ernst Neufert and his teaching on building design – with extensive consequences, especially in postwar modernity. Simple and economic constructions became the model for architects and designers throughout the 20th century and beyond.

Yet ornamentation did not disappear completely. Screening facades, often seemingly smooth and unadorned and illustrating an industrial aesthetic, certainly display patterns, which do not follow the technical constructions at all. Mies van der Rohe's Seagram Building is said to have an "ornamental" facade. For the highrise, with its screening facade, receives its soaring character through vertical double T-girders made of bronze, which are applied to the facade. The bearing structure lies inside the building and is hence, at most, represented outwardly.[11] Widely differing authors point, with great unanimity, to this form of scarcely perceived décor in modern architecture. Brent C. Brolin's book on the architectural ornament bears the subtitle "Banishment and Return"[12] – on the basis of a rathermore traditional concept of ornamentation and décor this and other modern examples are there explained as signposts to postmodernity. The enthusiasm of Robert Venturi and Denise Scott Brown[13] for Las Vegas and its "decorated sheds" then led to a return of ornamentation and of patterns in postmodern architecture and design. Above all in the sense of ironic quotations, columns, decorative gables, striped facades suddenly reappeared. But, although new patterns or décors were only rarely designed, postmodernity laid the basis for a new architectural complexity.[14] It was on this that the tendency to the new opulence in patterns could flourish best. Finally, an unconstrained treatment of patterns and images, which continues up to today and would have its origin in Las Vegas, joined the purely functional practices.[15]

Alongside their roots in postmodernity, there would be, of course, further motivations and influences behind the return of patterns in contemporary architecture. The tendency to extreme reduction, the minimalism of the 1990s, turned out to be a blind alley or, at least, did not lend itself to all construction commissions. Only the use of patterned facades achieved here, amid all the conceptual clarity and severity of the structures, the desired aesthetic multivalency.

The distrust vis-à-vis decorated surfaces now receded before a pleasure in opulence, about which Oscar Wilde had already written: "It is only shallow people who do not judge by appearances. The true mystery of the world is the visible, not the invisible."[16] On the technical level of architecture, computer-based production methods today enabled the production of extensive details and minimal series, which previously denoted an expensive luxury and only now permit a variety of design, which was long unthinkable. Finally and most important, their encounter with the arts influenced many architects. Without their example, many of the patterns displayed here are not conceivable. Even if facades are not autonomous artworks either: they inspire us to see and to think. Contemporary architects, who work with patterns, find themselves in a paradoxical situation. They do indeed follow the demands of Adolf Loos and of modernity for rational design, nevertheless they are aiding the breakthrough of the long suppressed decoration of surfaces. Yet today that does not count as a crime any more.

1   Adolf Loos, Ornament and Crime. Translation from Ludwig Münz and Gustav Künstler, Adolf Loos: Pioneer of Modern Architecture, (New York: 1966), pp. 226–227.
2   "Oriented towards the example of the mass media, photography and film, architecture itself becomes a productions machinery for image-sequences…" Jörg H. Gleiter, Rückkehr des Verdrängten [The Return of the Suppressed], (Dessau: 2002), p. 314.
3   Patterns are determined by the combination of individual motifs in a structure, mostly organised on a surface. Repetition is characteristic, in an adaptation of the basic elements too. In this, symmetry and rhythm are constants from which simple or complex patterns can be developed.
4   see Gerhard Mack, Eberswalde Library – Herzog & de Meuron (London: 2000).
5   "It is a fact that we take up architectural themes, which were buried and partially criminalised – like ornamentation, for instance." Herzog & de Meuron interviewed by Philip Ursprung, in: Herzog & de Meuron, Naturgeschichte [Natural History], (Montréal: 2002).
6   Adolf Loos, Ornament and Crime, Lecture 1908, in: Adolf Loos, Ornament and Crime. Selected Essays. (Studies in Austrian Literature, Culture, and Thought Translation Series: 1997).
7   In that he refers to Alois Riegl, who describes the origins of ornamentation in prehistorical and non-European cultures. See: Alois Riegl, Stilfragen [Questions of Style], ed. Friedrich Piel (Munich: 1977), pp. 22 ff. and 77 ff.
8   see María Ocón Fernández, Ornament und Moderne [Ornament and Modernity], Theoriebildung und Ornamentdebatte im deutschen Architekturdiskurs (1850–1939) (Berlin: 2004), p. 12 ff.
9   Le Corbusier, Towards a New Architecture (London: 1946), pp. 128–129.
10 María Ocón Fernández, Ornament und Moderne, p. 13.
11 "In a classical rhetorical technology, the hidden support structure appears in Mies' double T-girder as ornatus, this is, an element which exaggerates the pure support structure." Jörg H. Gleiter, Rückkehr des Verdrängten [The Return of the Suppressed] (Dessau: 2002), p. 215.
12 Brent C. Brolin, Architectural Ornament. Banishment and Return (New York: 2000).
13 Robert Venturi, Denise Scott-Brown, Steven Izenour, Learning from Las Vegas (Cambridge: 1978).
14 "Postmodern neohistoricism tries to regain the transparency of complexity, which was lost in the International Style, through a collage of historical styles and forms." Hannes Böhringer, Begriffsfelder [Areas of Concepts], (Berlin: 1985), p. 19.
15 "Yes. Sign is more important than mass. Or put it another way, as someone wrote of our approach recently: building, sign, art – they're all one." Relearning from Las Vegas, Robert Venturi in an Interview, in: Rem Koolhaas, Content (Cologne: 2004), p. 56.
16 Oscar Wilde, The picture of Dorian Gray (London: 1994), p. 30.

Bettina Allamoda
Institut du Monde Arabe Wallpaper, 2004
Digital print – pigment on adhesive paper, mixed media
View of installation Zwinger Galerie, Berlin
courtesy of Zwinger Galerie, Berlin

Bettina Allamoda
Institut du Monde Arabe Showroom, 2003
Digital print – pigment on adhesive paper, mixed media
K & K – Zentrum für Kunst und Mode, Weimar
Exterior view

Bettina Allamoda
Institut du Monde Arabe Showroom, 2003
Interior view
Series of photographies, documentation
above: IMA John Galliano Showroom/Handbags, 2000
below: IMA John Galliano Showroom/Catwalk, 2001

Bettina Allamoda
Institut du Monde Arabe Showroom, 2003
Interior view
Series of photographies, documentation
above: IMA Sonia Rykiel Showroom, 2001
below: IMA John Galliano Showroom, 2001

Alsop Design Ltd.

Sharp Centre for Design Ontario, 2004

Steel frame building with aluminium covering
above: View to the south
below: View to the east

25 **Alsop Design Ltd.**
Sharp Centre for Design Ontario, 2004
Exterior view by night

Alsop Design Ltd.

Fawood Children's Centre London, 2005

Wire mesh casing with acrylic elements
below left: Detail east facade
below right: Detail south facade

27 **Alsop Design Ltd.**
Colorium Office Building Düsseldorf, 2001
Glass with colour printing
Exterior view

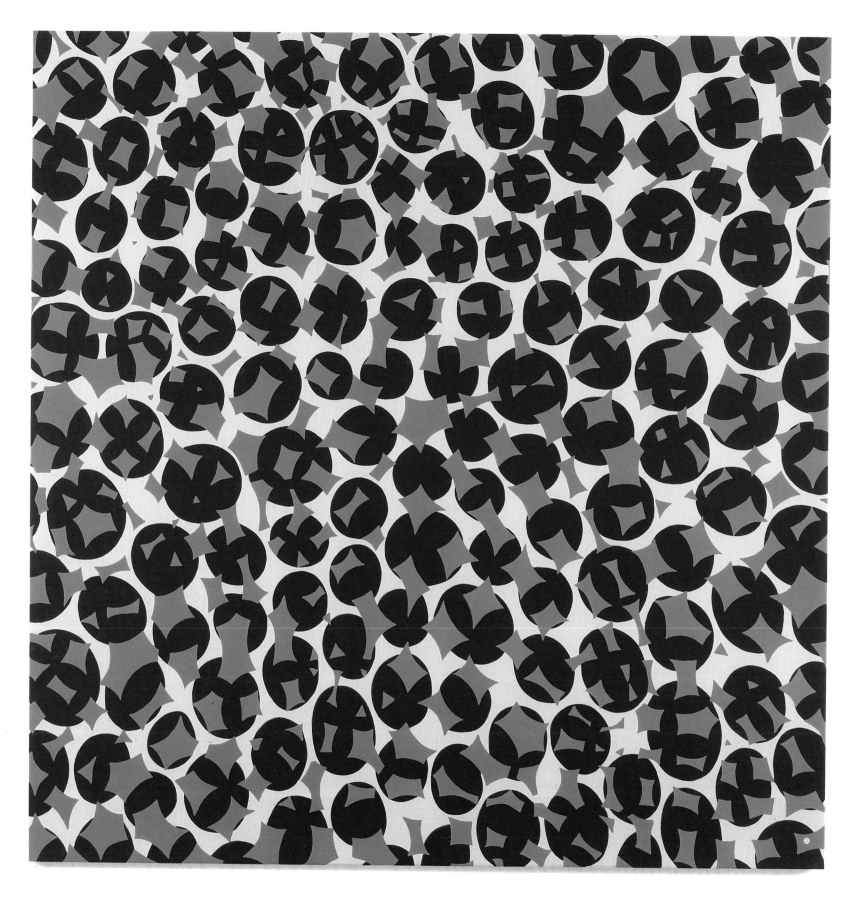

Birgit Antoni
Spacy 1 and Spacy 2, 2004
Oil and wax on canvas
2 parts, 135 x 135 cm each

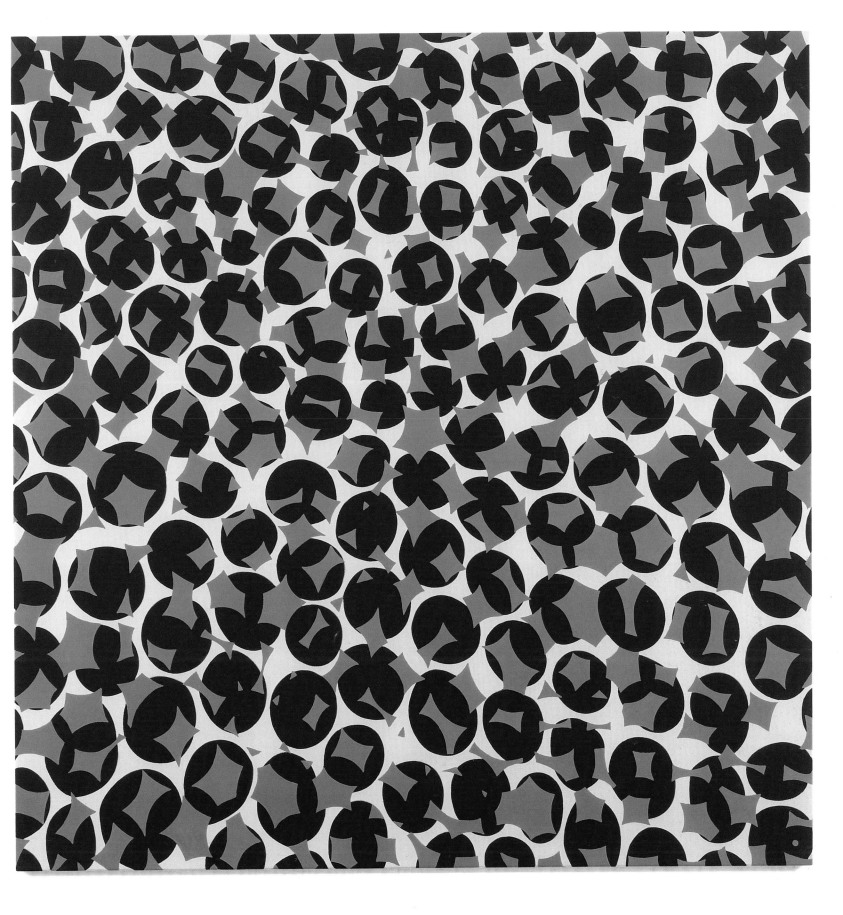

30

Birgit Antoni
Schleuderball 1 und Schleuderball 2 [Sling-ball 1 and Sling-ball 2],
2005

Oil and wax on canvas
2 parts, 135 x 135 cm each

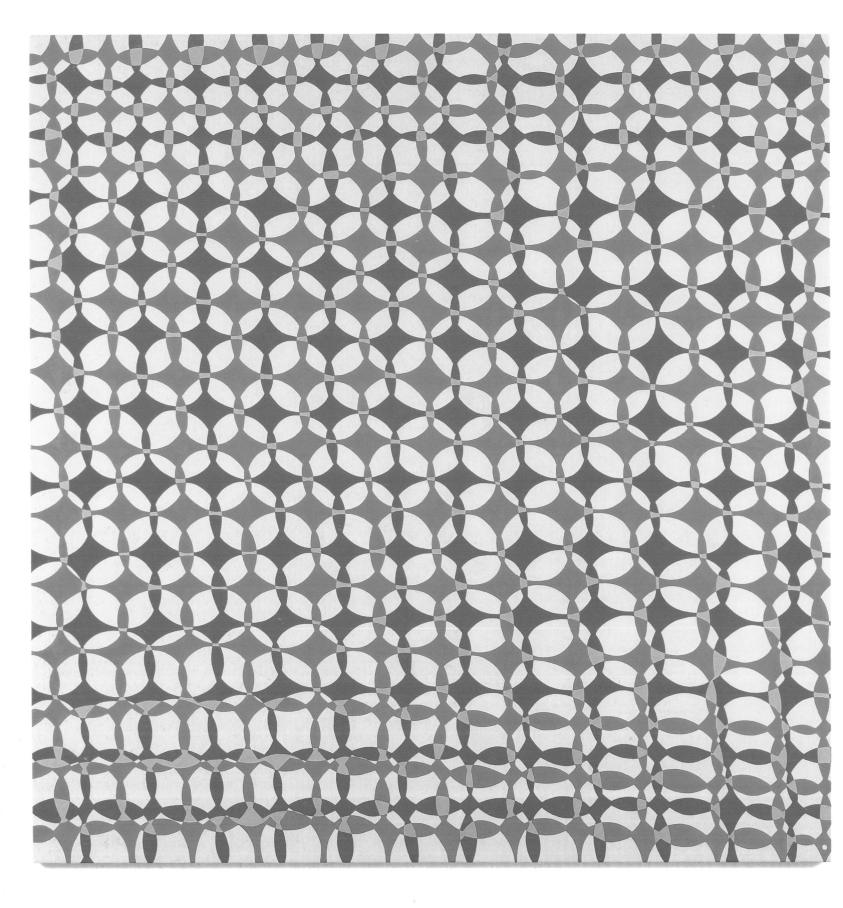

32 **Birgit Antoni**
Rosenrot mit Rosenrot [Roseate with Roseate], 2002
Oil and wax on canvas
2 parts, 163 x 163 cm each

34   **Haleh Anvari**
Chadornama I, 2004
Series of photographs
Digital prints

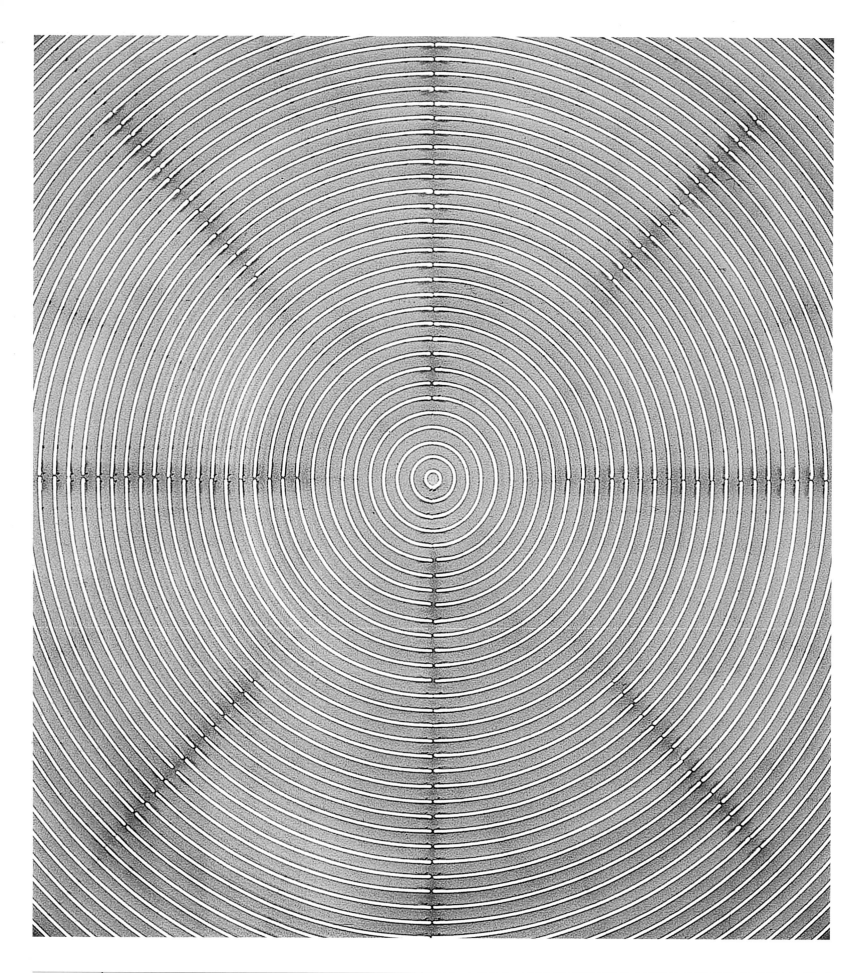

36

John M Armleder
Voltes IV, 2004 (Detail)

Neon
650 x 600 cm
courtesy of Caratsch de Pury & Luxembourg, Zurich

John M Armleder
Voltes IV, 2004
Neon
650 x 600 cm
courtesy of Caratsch de Pury & Luxembourg, Zurich

John M Armleder
Arsenic, 2003
Acrylic on canvas
300 x 200 cm
courtesy of Caratsch de Pury & Luxembourg, Zurich

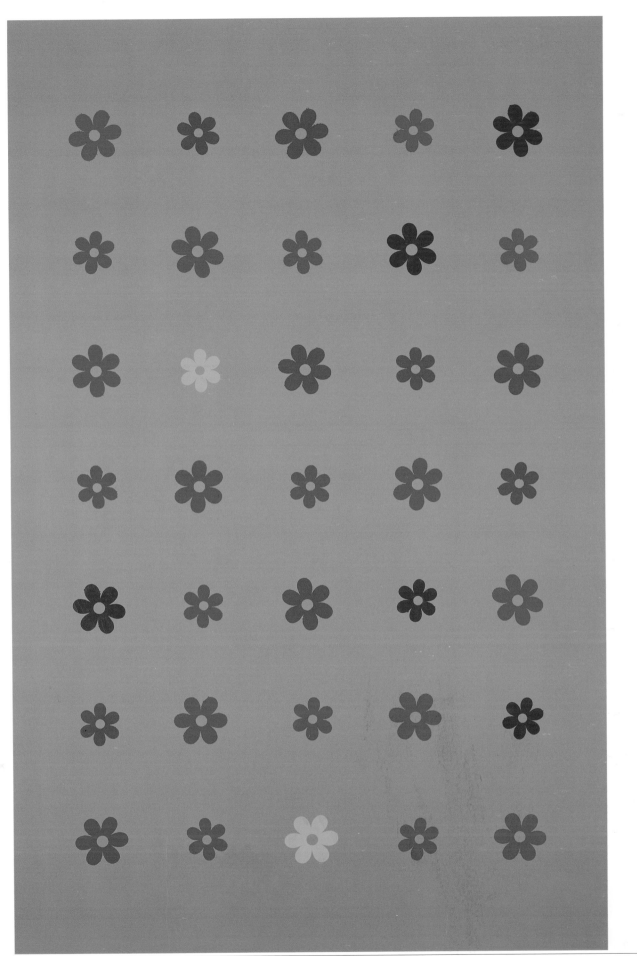

39   **John M Armleder**

Anthophyllite, 2004

Acrylic on canvas
300 x 200 cm
courtesy of Caratsch de Pury & Luxembourg, Zurich

40

Atelier Tekuto
Cell Brick Residential Building Tokyo, 2004
Ceramic coated steel elements
Exterior view by night

41 | **Atelier Tekuto**
Cell Brick Residential Building Tokyo, 2004
Interior view ground floor

42 **Baumschlager & Eberle**
Münchner Rück Office Building Munich, 2002
Foyer with maple parquet

Baumschlager & Eberle
Münchner Rück Office Building Munich, 2002
above: Café area with bar
below: Internal bridge first floor

Thomas Bayrle
Mäntel vor Schuhraster [Coats in front of a grid of shoes], 1967
Screen-print on paper, screen-print on synthetic material
Galleria Apollinaire, Milan, 1968

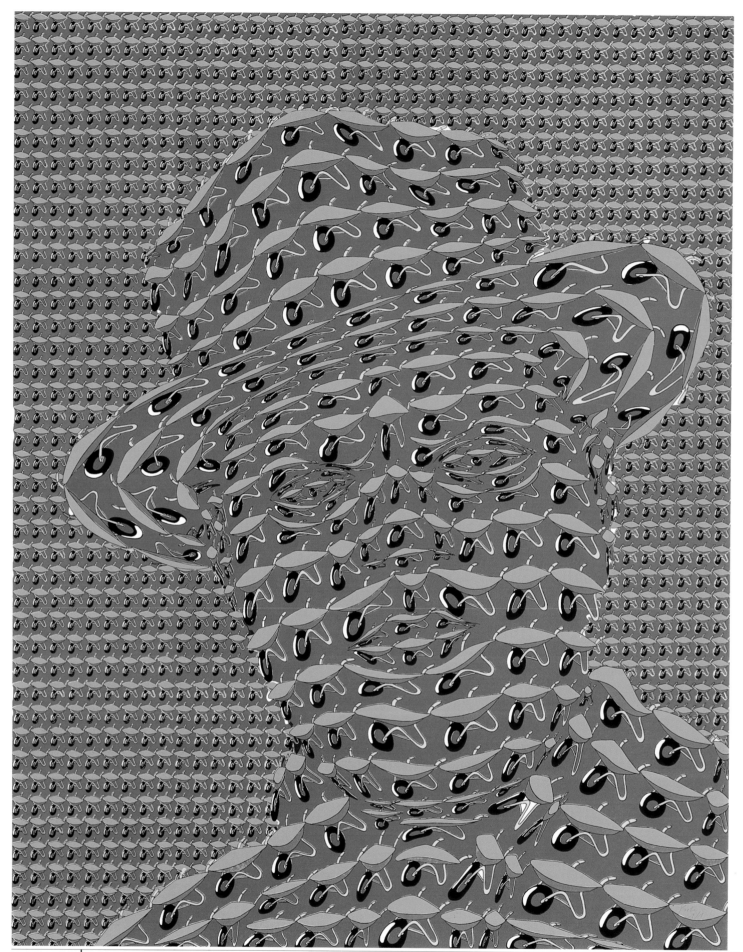

46 **Thomas Bayrle**

Orson Welles, 1971

Silkscreen on paper
76 x 60.5 cm
courtesy of Galerie Barbara Weiss, Berlin

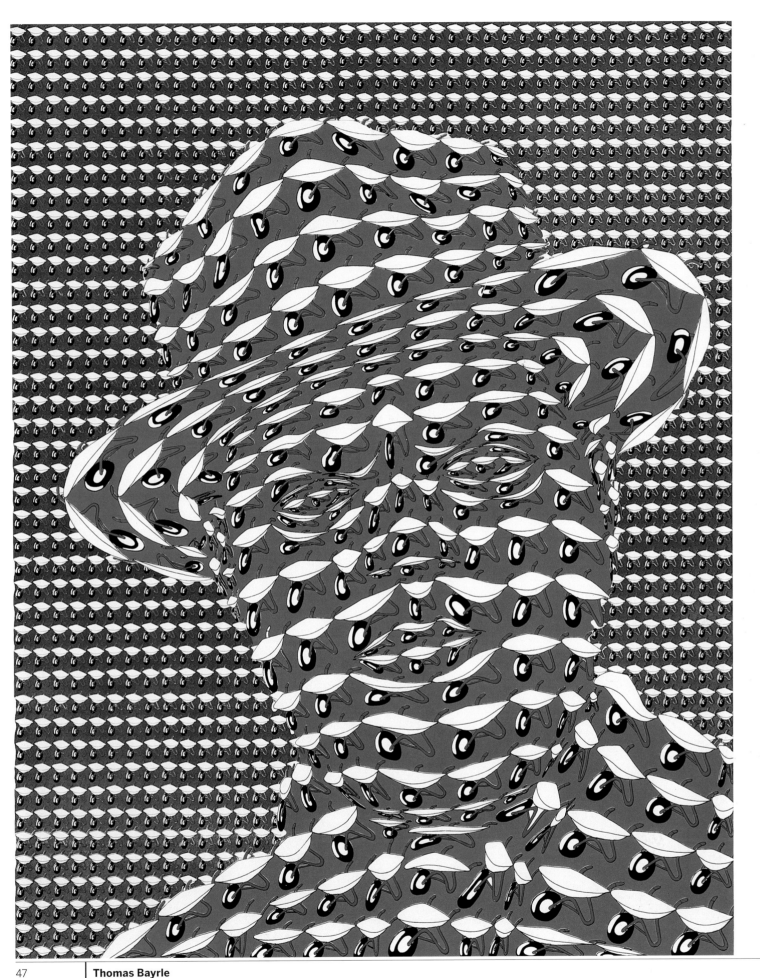

47

Thomas Bayrle

Orson Welles, 1971

Silkscreen on paper
76 x 60,5 cm
courtesy of Galerie Barbara Weiss, Berlin

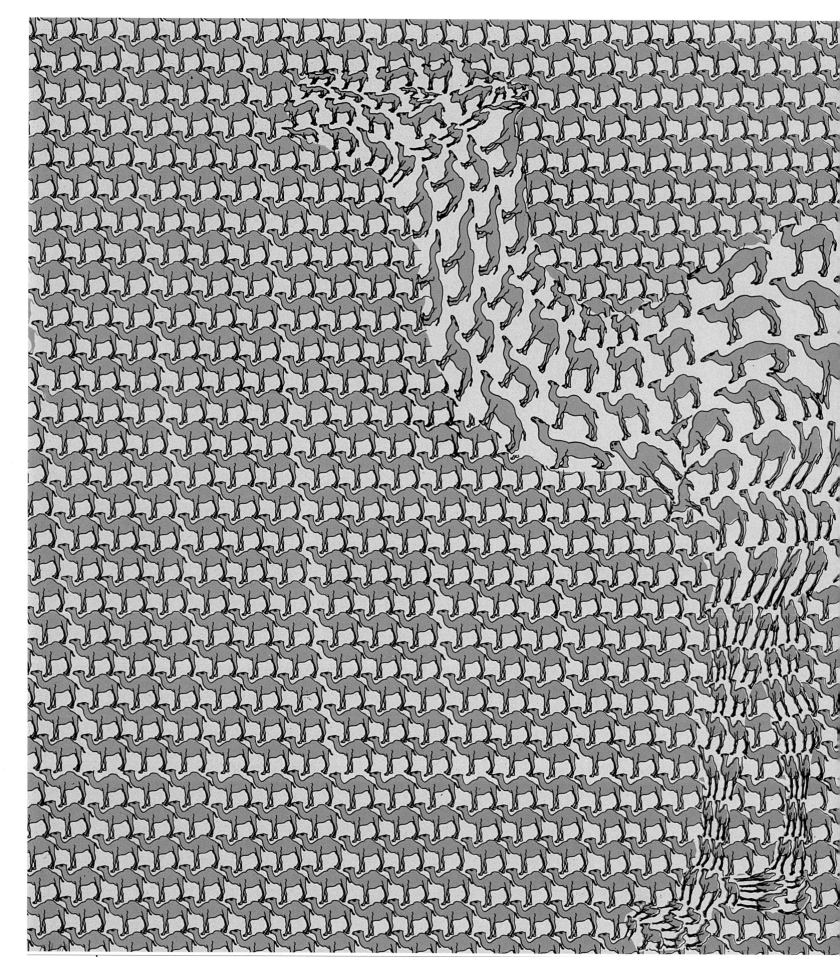

48

Thomas Bayrle
Camel, 1970

Silkscreen on paper
52 x 95,5 cm
courtesy of Galerie Barbara Weiss, Berlin

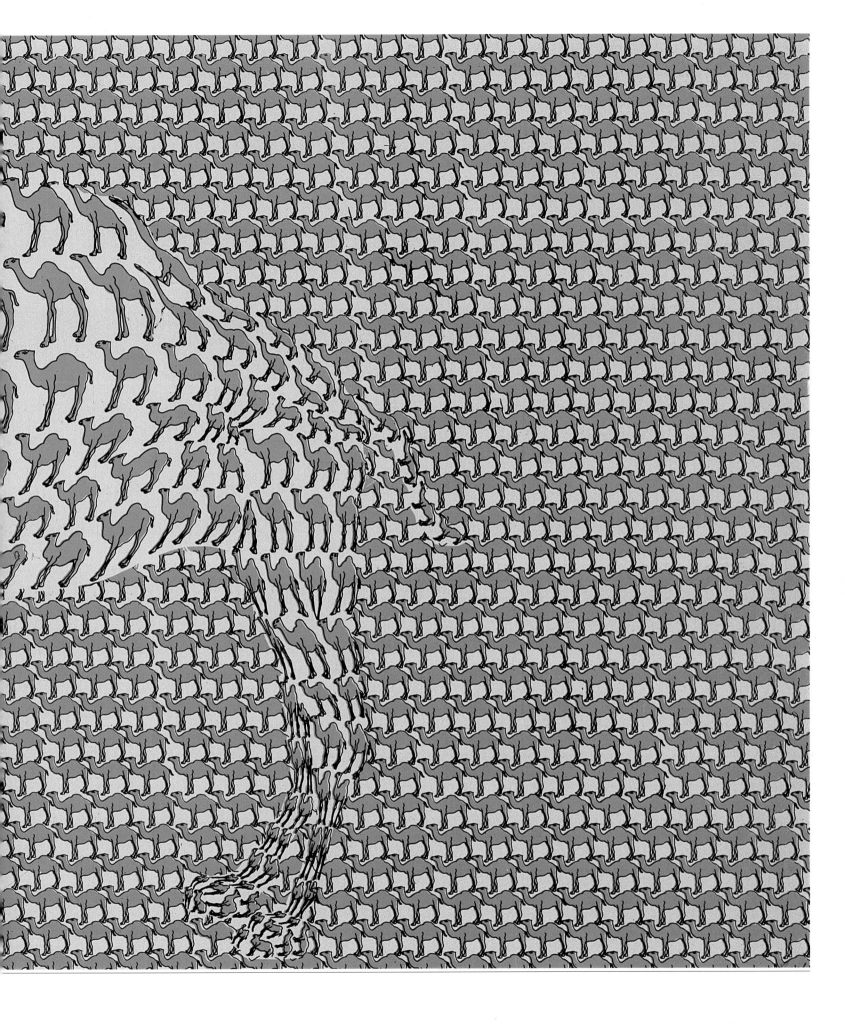

Vanessa Beecroft
Ponti Sister, June 30, 2001
Performance at Associazione Culturale Vista Mare, Pescara
Digital C-Print
courtesy of the artist and Deitch Projects, New York

Vanessa Beecroft

Ponti Sister, June 30, 2001

Performance at Associazione Culturale Vista Mare, Pescara
Digital C-Print
courtesy of the artist and Deitch Projects, New York

54 | **Jurgen Bey**
Interpolis, 2004
Various fabrics
Entrance hall Interpolis, Tilburg

Jurgen Bey
St. Petersburg Chairs, 2003
Antique chairs, PVC foam, fibre-glass reinforced polyester, screen-print
Café Dutch Room, St. Petersburg
Manufacturer: Droog Design

Tord Boontje

Princess Chair, 2004

Printed fabric, embroidery, metal plating
and leather
Manufacturer: Moroso

in the background:

Dondola, 2004

Steel frame chair with polyurethane foam cushioning:
Cover: Wool felt padding
Manufacturer: Moroso

Tord Boontje
Witch Chair, 2004
Steel frame chair with polyurethane foam cushioning,
leather strips stitched onto technical fabric
Manufacturer: Moroso

Tord Boontje
Princess, 2005
Upholstery fabric, screen-print on wool
Manufacturer: Kvadrat

59 **Tord Boontje**
Shadow, 2005
Curtain fabric, digital printing on polyester
Manufacturer: Kvadrat

Tord Boontje
Garland Light, 2002
Photographically etched metal
Manufacturer: Habitat

61 **Tord Boontje**
Wall Hanging, 2004
Lasercut microfibre
Manufacturer: Moroso

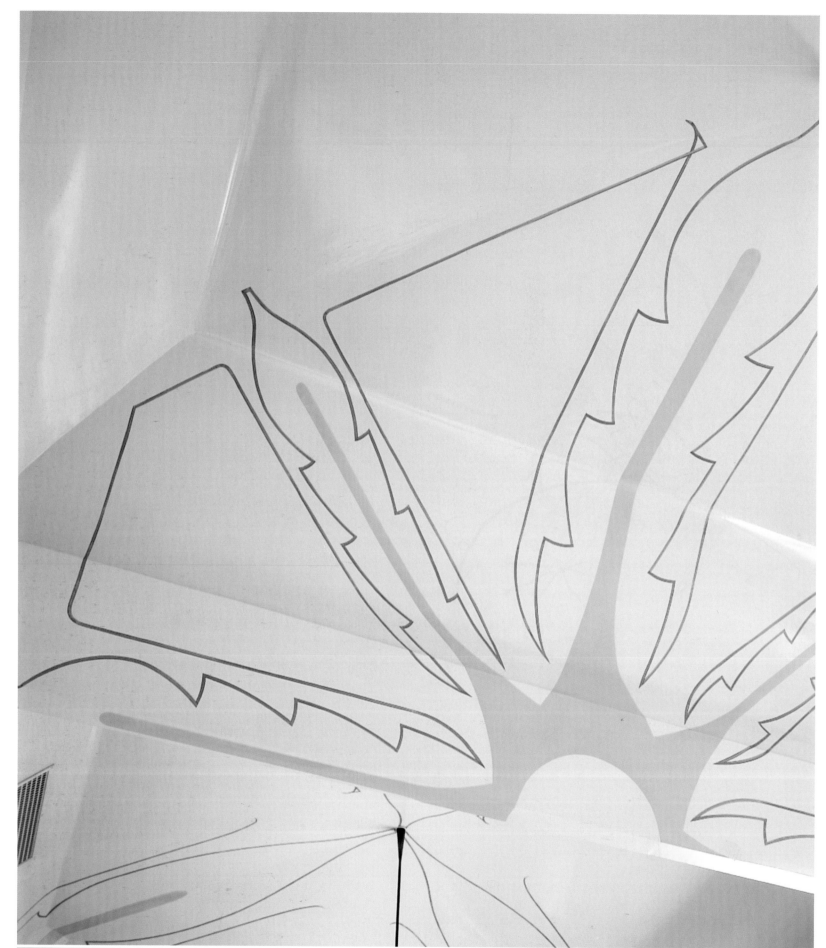

Bosshard Vaquer Architekten
Alteration Funeral Parlour Sihlfeld, 2004
Detail of mural painting

63   **Bosshard Vaquer Architekten**
Alteration Funeral Parlour Sihlfeld, 2004

Addition to historic decoration
Interior view

Linda Bradford
Bermuda, 2005
Digital chromatic study
Series Strata Mandala

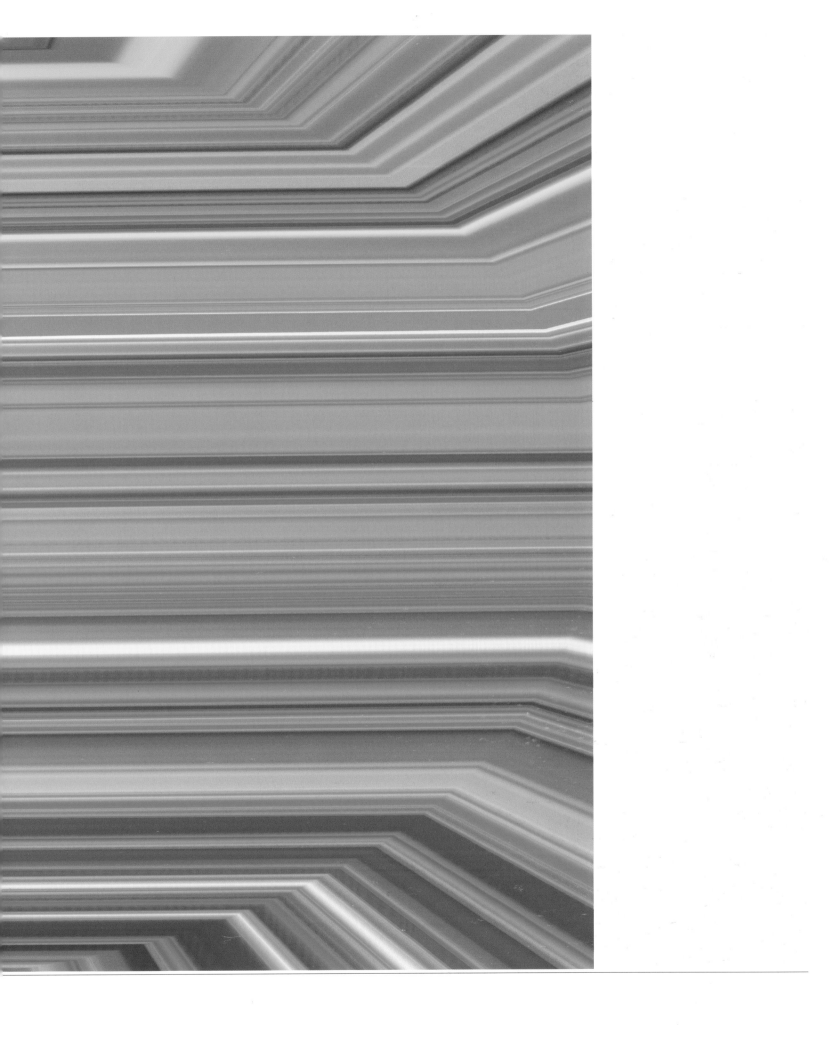

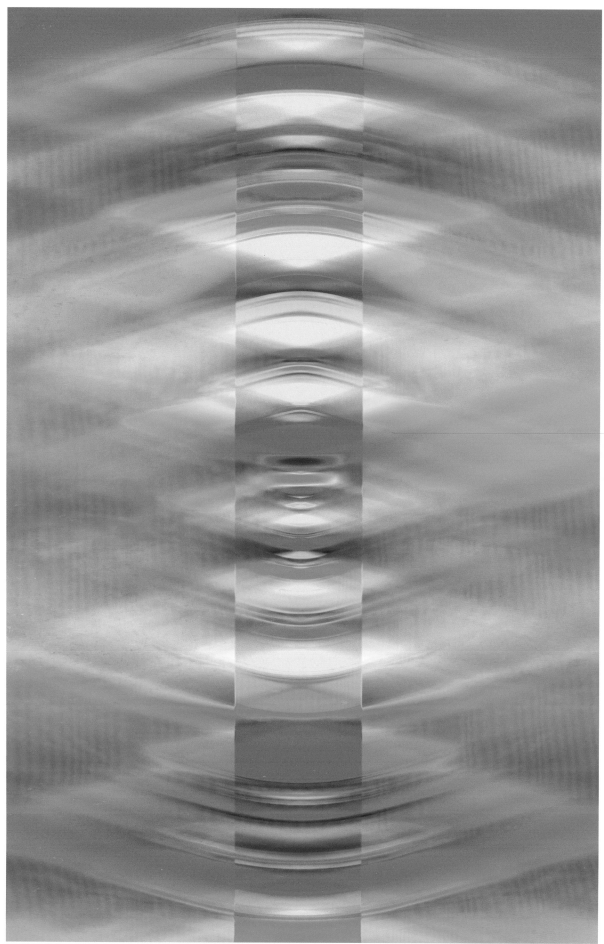

Linda Bradford
Totem, 2005
Digital chromatic study
Series Lumenations

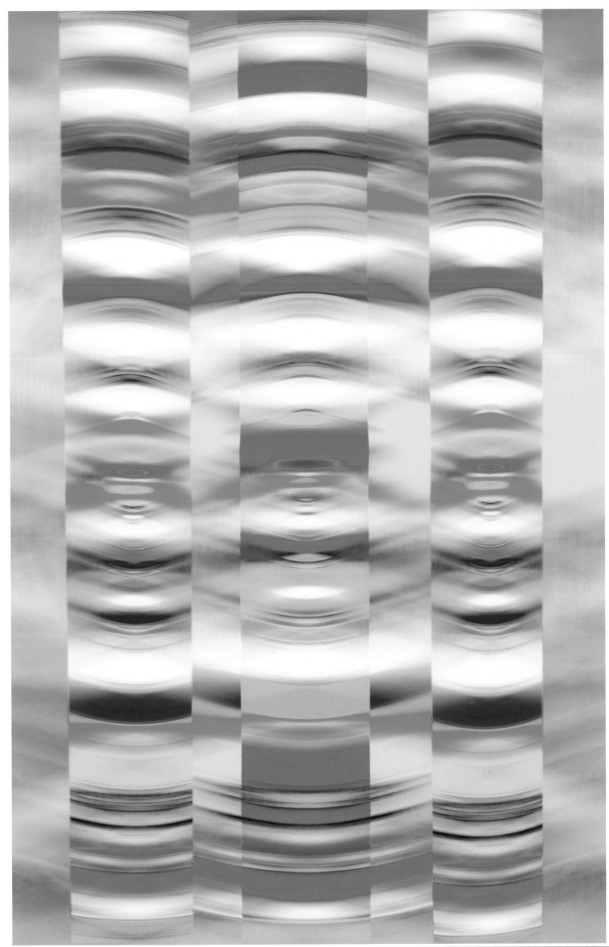

Linda Bradford
Trio, 2005
Digital chromatic study
Series Lumenations

Stefan Bressel
Quattro Stagioni, 2005
Distemper with fluorescent pigments on wall
Wallpainting
Exterior view Pavillon Schloss Molsberg/Emmanuel Walderdorff Galerie, Cologne

Stefan Bressel
Quattro Stagioni, 2005
Distemper with fluorescent pigments on wall
Wallpainting
View of installation Pavillon Schloss Molsberg/Emmanuel Walderdorff Galerie,
Cologne

Stefan Bressel

Hotel/bordeaux, 2002

Walldrawing, coloured marker on wall
View of installation
Galerie Hartmut Beck, Erlangen

left wall:

Smart Painting No. 8,
2001

Oil and acrylic on canvas
2 parts, 127,6 x 87 cm each

right wall top:

Smart Painting No. 6,
2001

Oil and acrylic on canvas
2 parts, 62 x 57,5 cm each

right wall bottom:

Smart Painting No. 7,
2001

Oil and acrylic on canvas
2 parts, 36,5 x 43,5 cm each

floor:

Zebra, 2002

MDF, acrylic, ink, aluminium
profile
ca. 220 x 150 cm

71 | **Stefan Bressel**
Hotel/grau [Hotel/grey], 2003
(Detail)

Wall drawing, coloured marker on wall
View of installation Galerie Perpetuel,
Frankfurt/Main

ohne Titel [Untitled], 2003

Oil and casein paint on canvas
2 parts, 38 x 34 cm each

Persijn Broersen & Margit Lukács
Black Light, 2004
Wall covering
View of installation Nieuwe Vide Gallery, Haarlem

Persijn Broersen & Margit Lukács
Black Light, 2004 (Details)
Wall covering
View of installation Nieuwe Vide Gallery, Haarlem

Stefanie Bürkle

Berliner Tapete [Berlin Wallpaper]

Office of Daniel Barenboim, General Music Director at the State Opera
Unter den Linden, Berlin
Wallpaper from 11.11.2003 onwards

Stefanie Bürkle
Berliner Tapete [Berlin Wallpaper]
Office of Peter Conradi, President of the Federal Association of Architects, Berlin
(until 2004)
Wallpaper from 28.07.2003 until 21.10.2004

Stefanie Bürkle

Berliner Tapete [Berlin Wallpaper]

Office of Hortensia Völckers, Artistic Director of the
Federal Cultural Foundation, Berlin
Wallpaper from 29.10.2003 until 12.11.2003

79 **Stefanie Bürkle**
Berliner Tapete [Berlin Wallpaper]
Office of Klaus Biesenbach, Director of Kunst-Werke [Institute for
Contemporary Art], Berlin
Wallpaper from 29.10.2003 until 6.11.2003

Stefanie Bürkle
Berliner Zimmer [Berlin Room]
Student Cafeteria/Dept. of Town Planning at the Technical University of Berlin
Wallpaper from March 2005 onwards

Stefanie Bürkle
Berliner Tapete [Berlin Wallpaper]
Bar KM 36, Berlin Mitte
Wallpaper from 04.02.2004 until June 2004

82 **Claudia Caviezel**
tape it (blinds), 2002
Painter's masking tape stuck on window

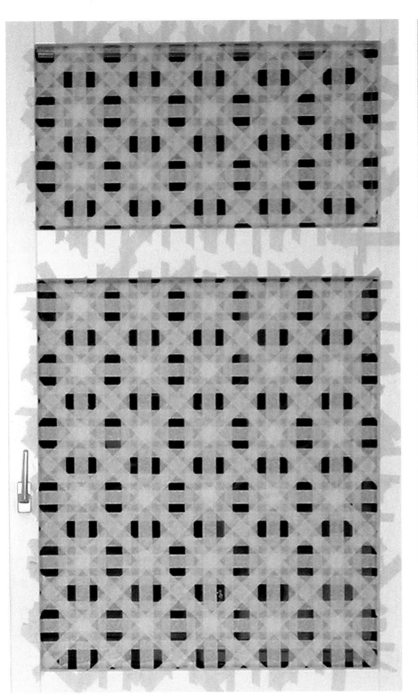

Chalet 5
sPaGaT 20050802_13:13, 2005
Silkscreen on inkjet print
55 x 66 cm

Chalet 5
sPaGaT 20050801_12:43, 2005
Photography, inkjet print, cardboard
75 x 95 cm

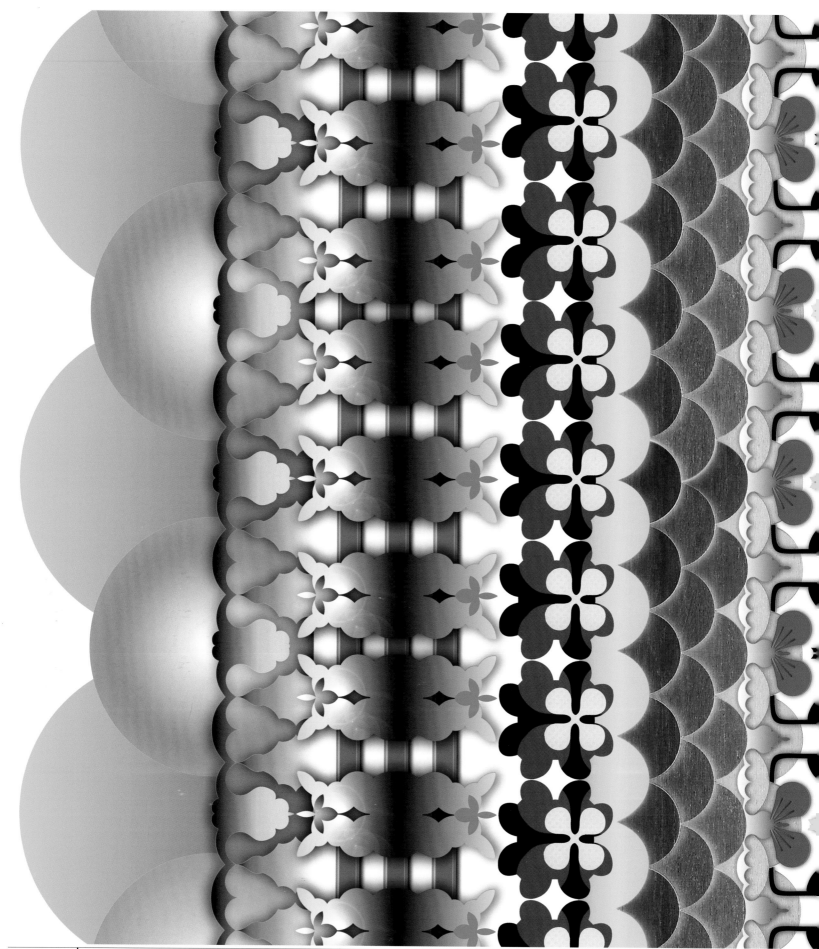

Chalet 5
East West, 2005
Study

Chalet 5
SpeedFresh, 2004
C-Print
90 x 120 cm

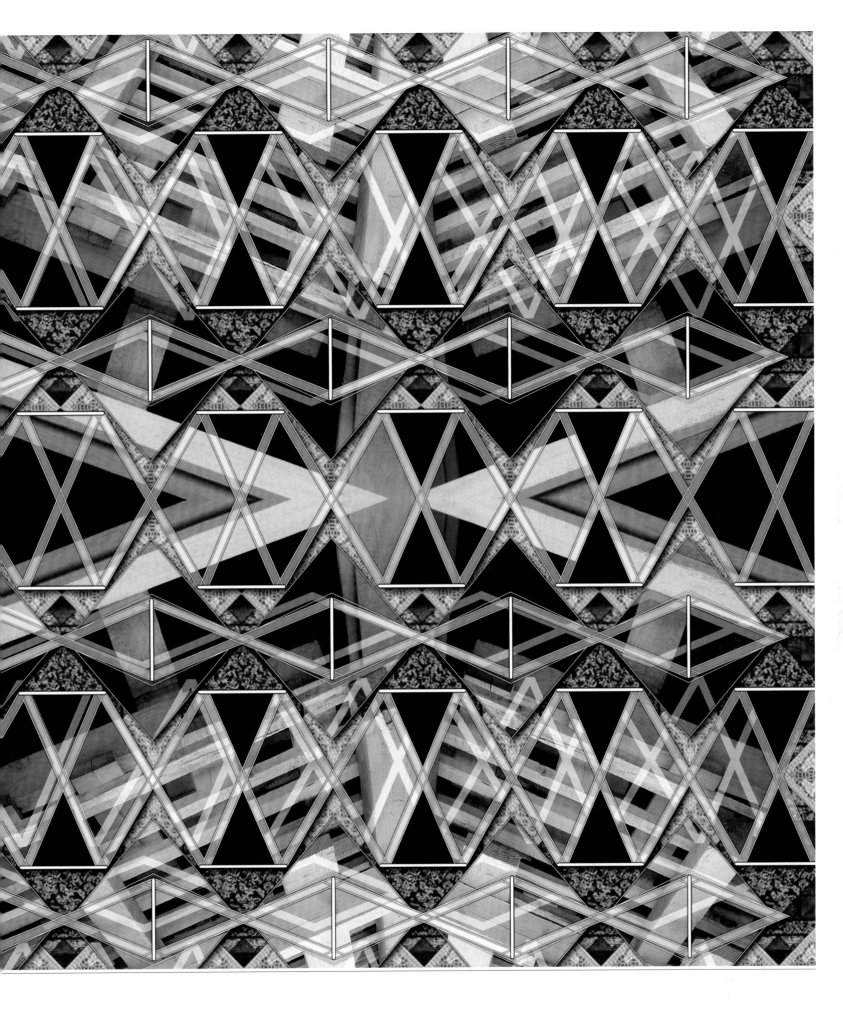

90
Claesson Koivisto Rune
Sfera Commercial Building Kyoto, 2003
Pierced titanium panels
Detail of facade

Claesson Koivisto Rune
Sfera Commercial Building Kyoto, 2003
Facade by night

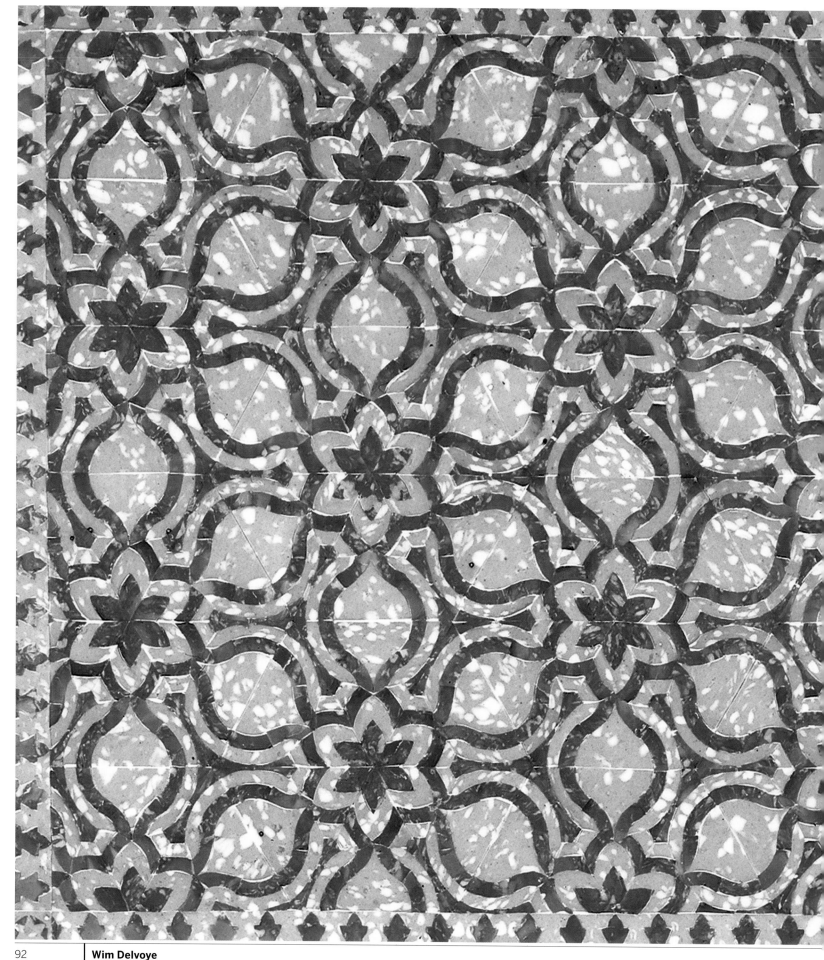

92

Wim Delvoye
Marble Floor # 103, 1999

Cibachrome print on aluminium
110 x 202 cm
courtesy of Sperone Westwater, New York

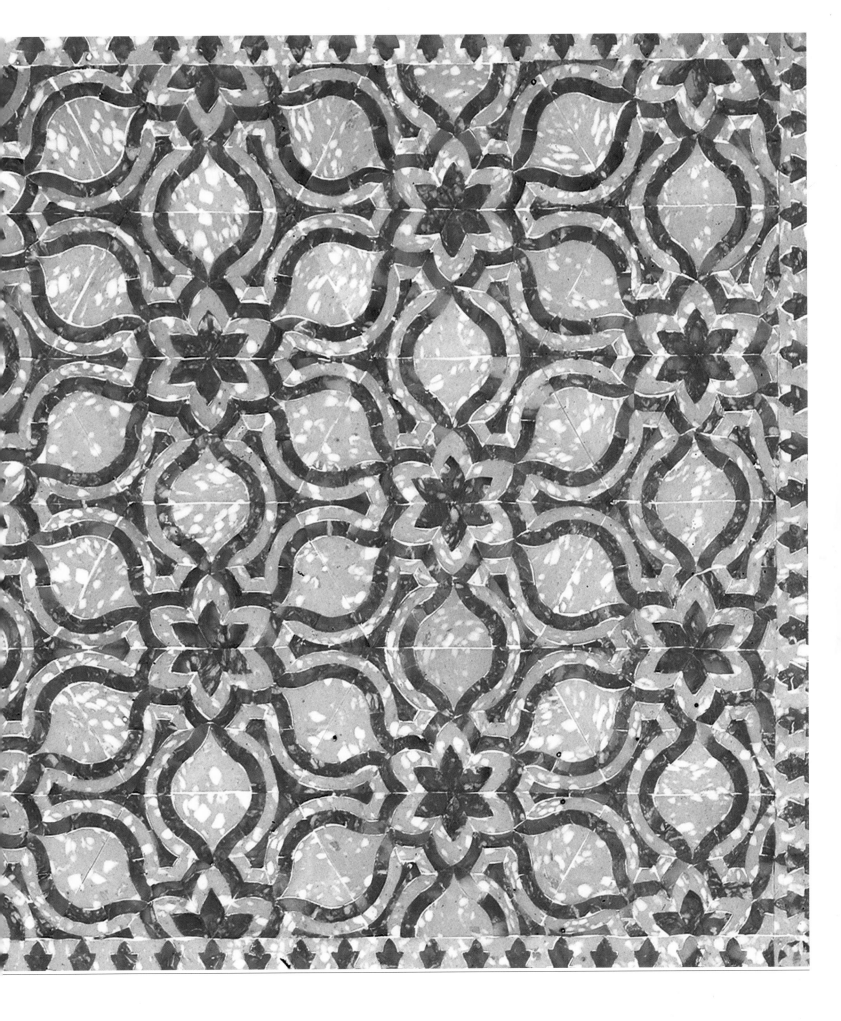

94   **Wim Delvoye**

Marble Floor # 111, 1999

Cibachrome print on aluminium
110 x 207 cm
courtesy of Sperone Westwater, New York

below:

Marble Floor # 87, 1999

Cibachrome print on aluminium
110 x 197 cm
courtesy of Sperone Westwater, New York

95 **Wim Delvoye**
Caterpillar #5, 2002

Laser cut corten steel
350 x 900 x 300 cm
View of installation Gothic, Public Art Fund Project
courtesy of Public Art Fund, New York

Erick van Egeraat Associated Architects
Municipal Building Alphen aan den Rijn, 2002
Screen-print on glass
below left: Interior view atrium
below right: Offices and service area of municipal building

Erick van Egeraat Associated Architects
Municipal Building Alphen aan den Rijn, 2002
Detail of facade in the evening

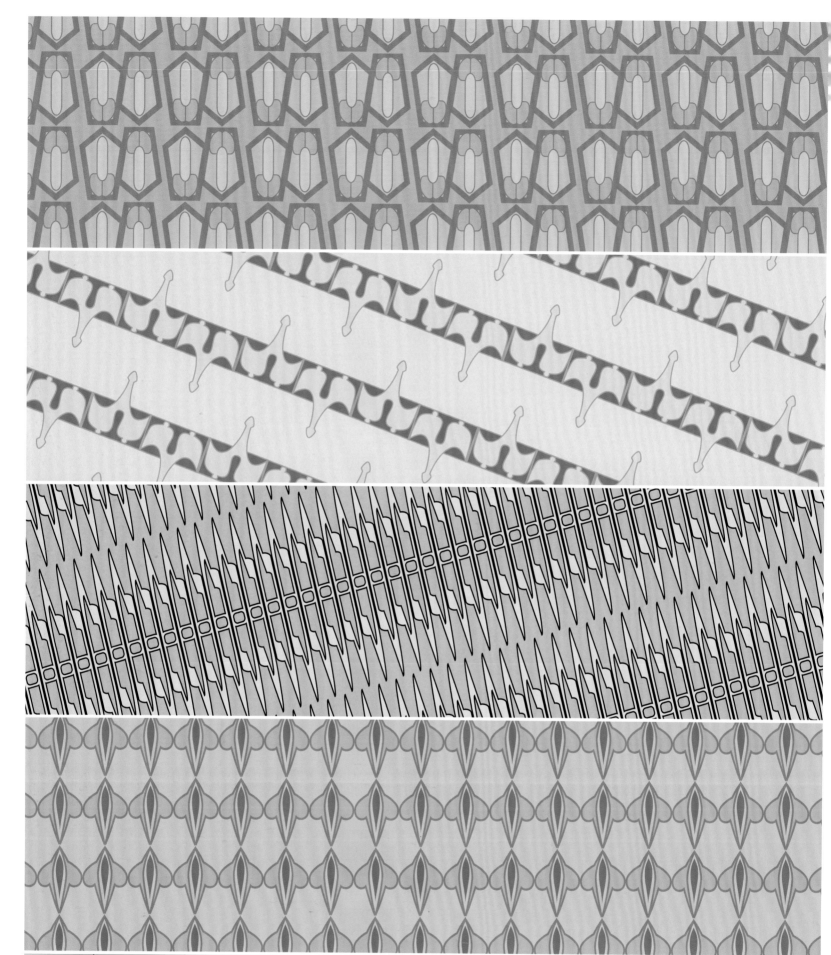

98

Parastou Forouhar
eslimi, 2003
Series Genital and Series Fork
Textile print

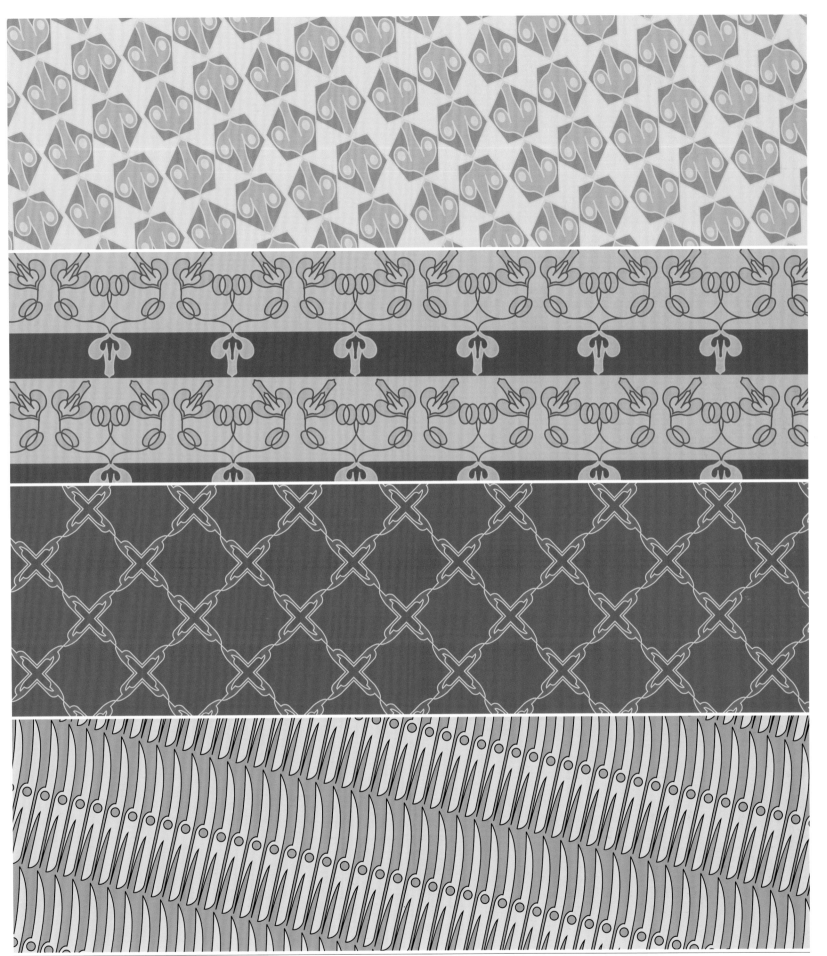

99

100 **Parastou Forouhar**
eslimi, 2003
Series Genital and Series Fork
Textile print

Future Systems

Selfridges Department Store Birmingham, 2003

Concrete facade with aluminium glazing
Exterior view by night

Future Systems
Selfridges Department Store Birmingham, 2003
Exterior view by day

Daan van Golden

Composition with Brown Square, 1964

Gloss paint on canvas on panel
70 x 70 cm
Rijksdienst Beeldende Kunst, The Hague
Loan to the Museum Boijmans Van Beuningen – State collection, Rotterdam

105 **Daan van Golden**

Composition with Roses, 1964

Gloss paint on canvas on framed panel
120 x 96 cm
Museum Boijmans Van Beuningen, Rotterdam

Klaus Haapaniemi
Here today, gone tomorrow, 2004
Silk embroidery on cotton
Manufacturer: Bantam

Klaus Haapaniemi
Smiling Man, 2004
Book illustration for Pocko (UK), Ginko Press (US)

Klaus Haapaniemi
Witch, 2004
Book illustration for Pocko (UK), Ginko Press (US)

Klaus Haapaniemi
Floral Top, 2004
Laser-cut lambswool-synthetic blend
Manufacturer: Bantam

Klaus Haapaniemi
Floral, 2004
Study
Manufacturer: Bantam

112

Elke Haarer

ohne Titel [Untitled], 2001

Foil plotting on glass
View of installation in the exhibition hall of the Akademie der Bildenden Künste
in Nürnberg [College of Fine Arts in Nuremberg]

114 **Elke Haarer**
Giverny, 2002
Offset printing, used as wallpaper
View of installation Kunstverein Kohlenhof, Nuremberg

Elke Haarer
Wallpaper, 2002
Study

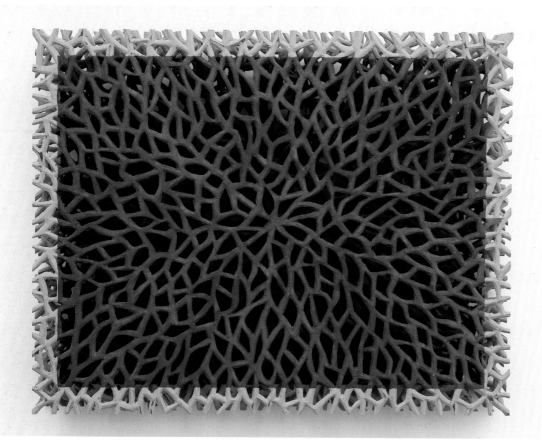

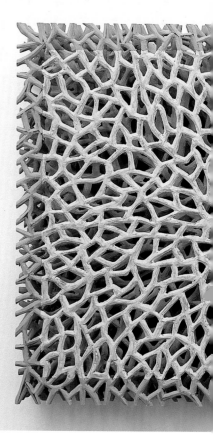

Tobias Hauser

Der Morgen [Morning], 2004
MDF, casein-tempera
100 x 130 x 18 cm
courtesy of Zwinger Galerie, Berlin

Der Tag [Day], 2004
MDF, casein-tempera
100 x 130 x 18 cm
courtesy of Zwinger Galerie, Berlin

Der Abend [Evening], 2004
MDF, casein-tempera
100 x 130 x 18 cm
courtesy of Zwinger Galerie, Berlin

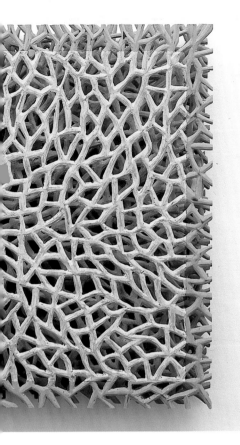
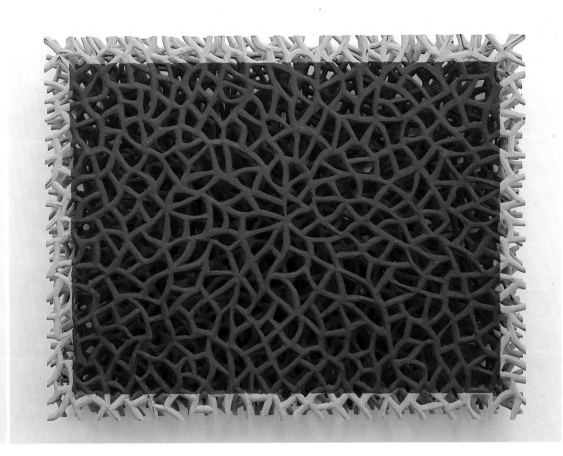

120 **Geka Heinke**
Baseballfeld [Baseball field], 2000
Gouache on wall
300 x 600 cm
View of installation Galerie Nord, Kunstamt Tiergarten/Mitte, Berlin

122

Geka Heinke

Dose [Can], 2001

Gloss paint and tempera on hardboard
170 x 150 cm

123 **Geka Heinke**
Vorhang schwarz-weiß [Curtain black-white], 2002
Tempera on hardboard
138 x 133 cm

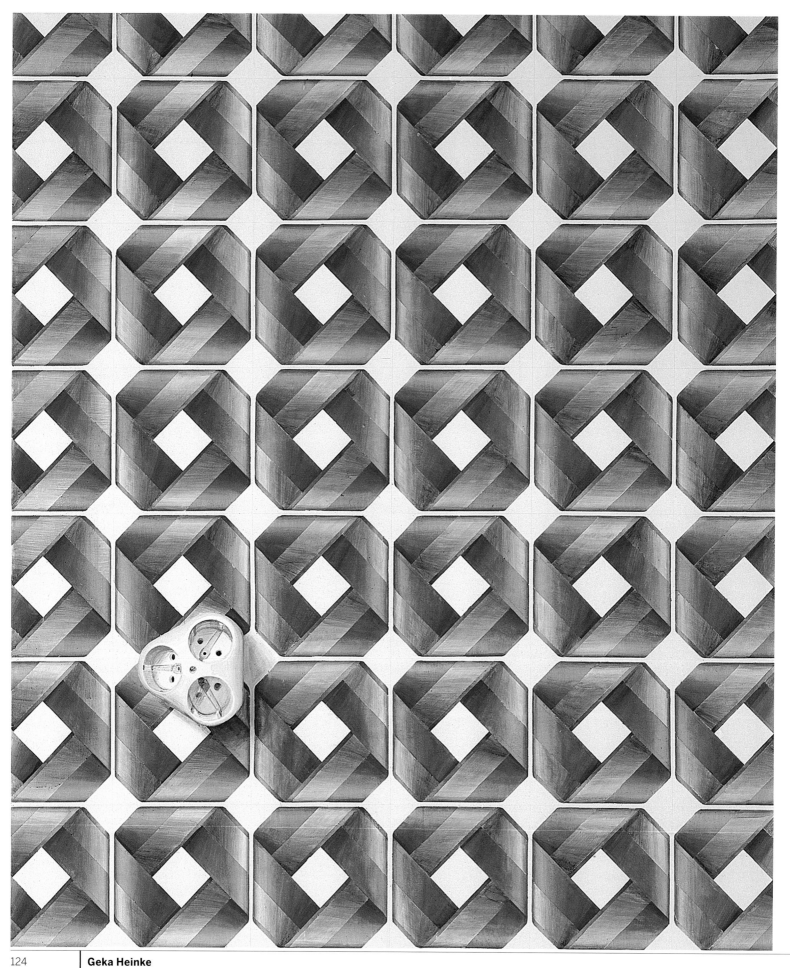

124   **Geka Heinke**
Tapete und Steckdose [Wallpaper and Socket], 2002
Acrylic and tempera on nettle-cloth
230 x 180 cm

125 **Geka Heinke**
Regal und Tapete [Shelf and Wallpaper], 2001
Tempera and oil on nettle-cloth
200 x 150 cm

Herzog & de Meuron
Library Eberswalde, 1999
Concrete relief, printed glass
Exterior view

Herzog & de Meuron
Library Eberswalde, 1999
Concrete relief, printed glass
Detail of facade

Hild und K
Residential Building Aggstal, 2000
Brickwork
Exterior view

129 **Hild und K**
Residential Building Aggstal, 2000
Detail of facade

Hild und K
Münchner Rück Interior Design Munich, 2001
Sgraffito technique
Detail of wall drawing in the conference room

131 **Hild und K**
Research Institute Munich, 2004
Varnish
Exterior view

Steven Holl Architects

Simmons Hall Residential Housing Cambridge, Massachusetts,
2002

Prefabricated concrete parts, anodized aluminium
Exterior view

Steven Holl Architects
Simmons Hall Residential Housing Cambridge, Massachusetts,
2002
Detail of facade

Steven Holl Architects

Simmons Hall Residential Housing Cambridge, Massachusetts, 2002

above: Interior view
below left: Living space
below right: Communal room

Toyo Ito & Associates, Architects
Performing Arts Center Matsumoto, 2004
Detail of metal wall

Toyo Ito & Associates, Architects
Performing Arts Center Matsumoto, 2004
Glass fibre strengthened concrete panels, glass elements
Exterior view

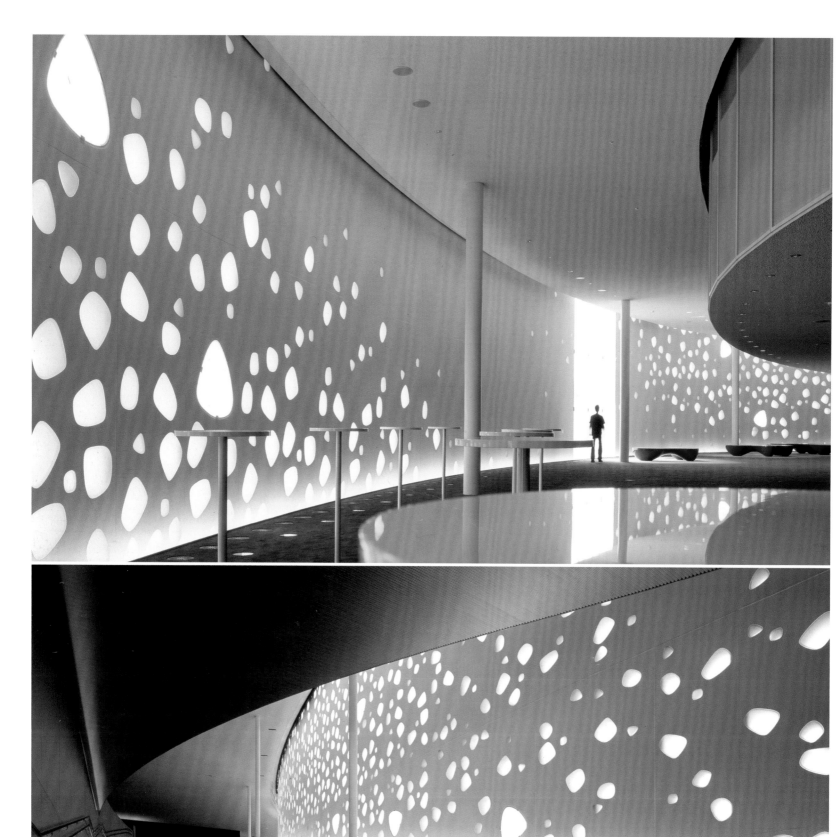

138 **Toyo Ito & Associates, Architects**
Performing Arts Center Matsumoto, 2004
above: Foyer
below: Stairs to foyer

Toyo Ito & Associates, Architects
Performing Arts Center Matsumoto, 2004
Detail of foyer

Emily Kngwarreye, Alalgura Country, 1994

140   **Dale Jones-Evans Architecture**

Artwall Commercial Building Darlinghurst, 2003

Steel elements
above: Detail of facade
below: Interior view

Acrylic on canvas, 152 x 121 cm

Emily Kngwarreye, Alalgura Country, 1994

141 **Dale Jones-Evans Architecture**
Artwall Commercial Building Darlinghurst, 2003
Exterior view

Hella Jongerius
Nymphenburg Sketches, 2004
Porcelain
Manufacturer: Nymphenburg Porcelain Manufactory, Munich

144 **Hella Jongerius**
Sampler Blankets, 2005
Wool
Collection Cooper-Hewitt National Design Museum, New York

Hella Jongerius
Repeat, 2002 (Detail)
Cotton, viscose
Manufacturer: Maharam

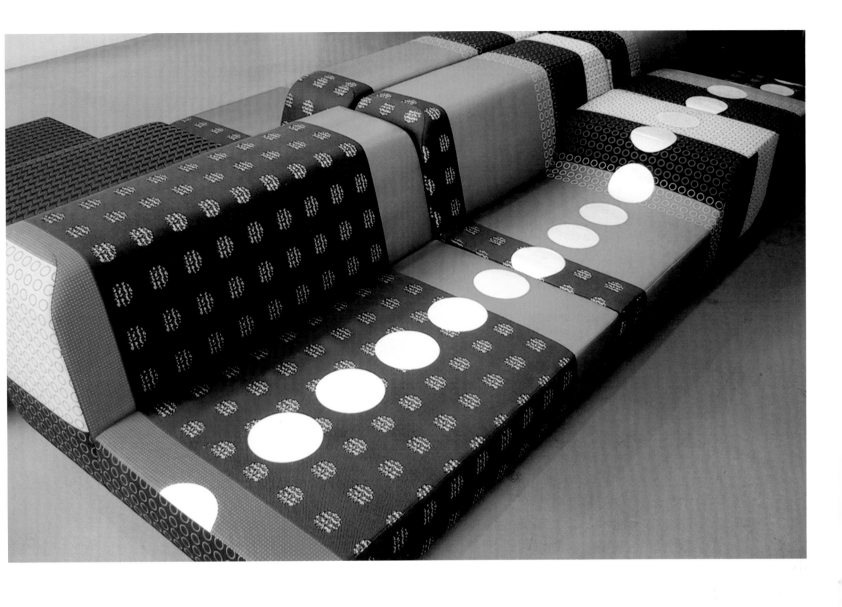

Hella Jongerius
Repeat, 2002
Cotton, viscose
Manufacturer: Maharam

Jourda Architectes

Manufacturing and Office Building Ebermannsdorf, 2002

Prefabricated concrete parts
Exterior view by night

Jourda Architectes
Manufacturing and Office Building Ebermannsdorf, 2002
Detail of facade

151 | **Jourda Architectes**
Manufacturing and Office Building Ebermannsdorf, 2002
Office building

152 **Klein Dytham Architecture**
Wedding Chapel Kobuchizawa, 2004
Perforated steel and acrylic lenses
above: Chapel by night
below: Influx of light through hole pattern by day

153

Klein Dytham Architecture
Wedding Chapel Kobuchizawa, 2004
above: Chapel by day, open
below: Detail of acrylic back supports

Silvia Knüppel & Damien Regamey
Homesick, 2005
Table tennis model
Machine made polyester-cotton weave

155 **Silvia Knüppel & Damien Regamey**

Homesick, 2005

Volleyball model
Polyester-weave, hand crocheting

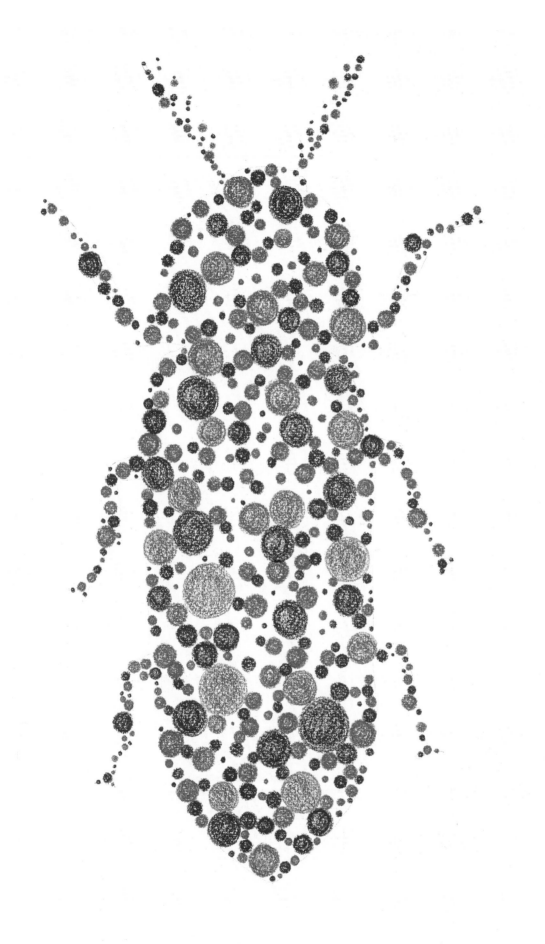

Takehito Koganezawa

Superficial Blackhole, 2002

Coloured pencil on paper
12 parts, 42 x 29,7 cm each
courtesy of Galerie Wohnmaschine, Berlin
Kenneth L. Freed collection, Boston

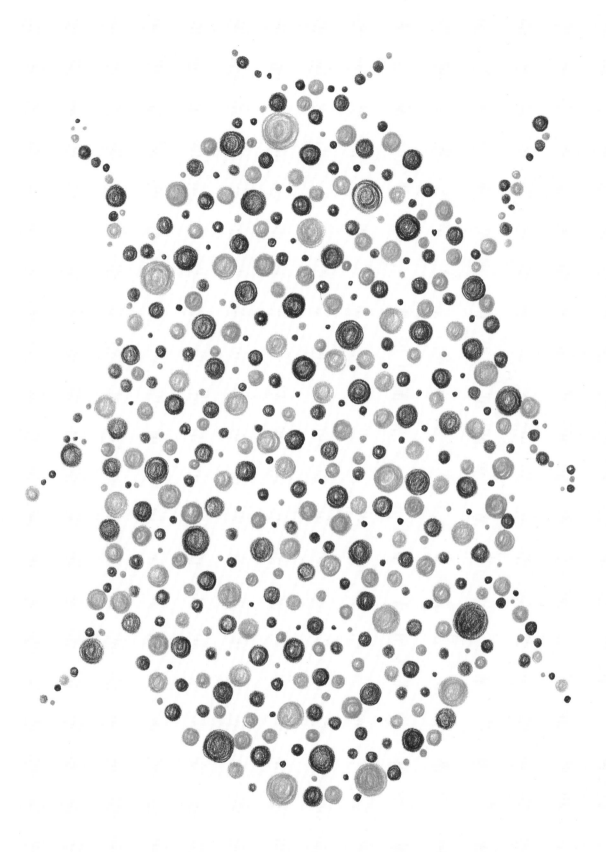

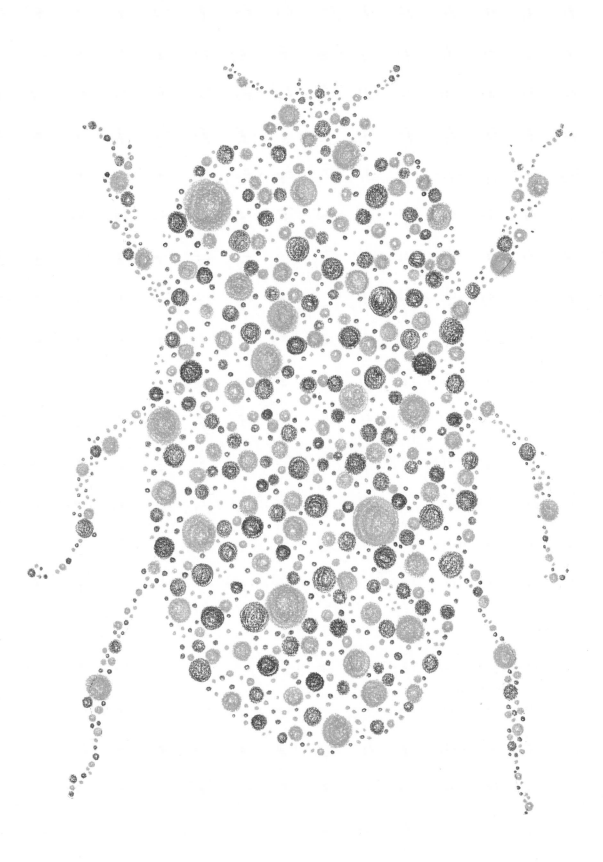

Takehito Koganezawa

Superficial Blackhole, 2002

Coloured pencil on paper
12 parts, 42 x 29,7 cm each
courtesy of Galerie Wohnmaschine, Berlin
Kenneth L. Freed collection, Boston

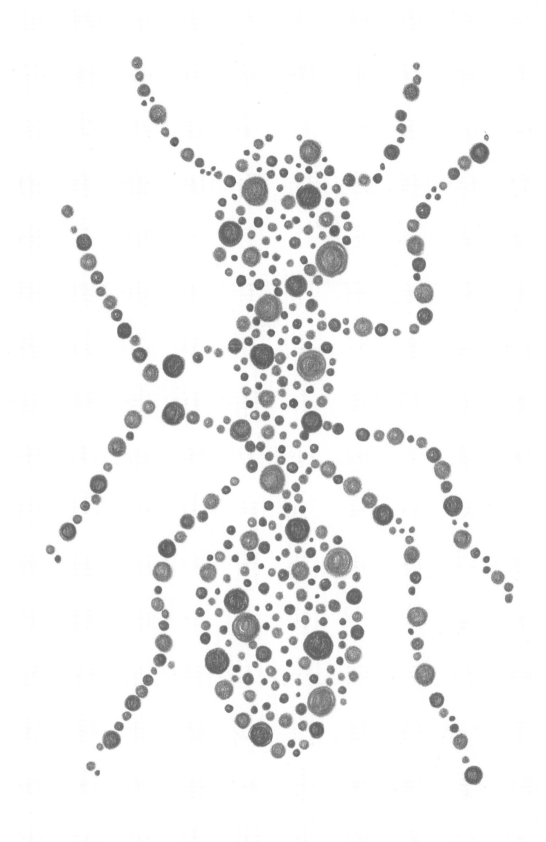

Peter Kogler
ohne Titel [Untitled], 2000
Computeranimation/projection
Sound: Franz Pomassl
View of installation Kunsthaus Bregenz

162   **Yayoi Kusama**
Dots Obsession, 1999
View of installation Kunstverein Braunschweig 2004

164 **Yayoi Kusama**
Video Room, 2004
View of installation Kunstverein Braunschweig 2004

166 **Lab Architecture Studio**
Federation Square Melbourne, 2002
Sandstone, zinc sheeting, glass
Partial view of square

Lab Architecture Studio
Federation Square Melbourne, 2002
Interior view south atrium

168   **Lab Architecture Studio**
Federation Square Melbourne, 2002
Detail of facade National Gallery of Victoria

Lab Architecture Studio
Federation Square Melbourne, 2002
Exterior view National Gallery of Victoria

Rüdiger Lainer
Residential Building Cobenzlgasse Vienna, 2004
Cast aluminium lattice
Exterior view

Rüdiger Lainer
Residential Building Cobenzlgasse Vienna, 2004
Detail of facade

Rüdiger Lainer

Office and Fitness Centre Hütteldorferstraße Vienna, 2003

Covering made of cast aluminium slabs
Exterior view

Rüdiger Lainer
Office and Fitness Centre Hütteldorferstraße Vienna, 2003
Facade elements

Abigail Lane
Volcanic Eruption/Fireplace, 2003
Chimney: flagstones: Wallpaper: coated inkjet printing
Manufacturer: Showroom Dummies

Abigail Lane
Electric Storm/Dog, 2003
Wallpaper: coated inkjet printing; Plaid: lambswool, cashmere
Manufacturer: Showroom Dummies

Abigail Lane

Skeleton, 2003

Wallpaper: screen-print; Chairs: black walnut, digitally printed fabric
Manufacturer: Showroom Dummies

Abigail Lane
Skeleton, 2003
Wallpaper: screen-print
Manufacturer: Showroom Dummies

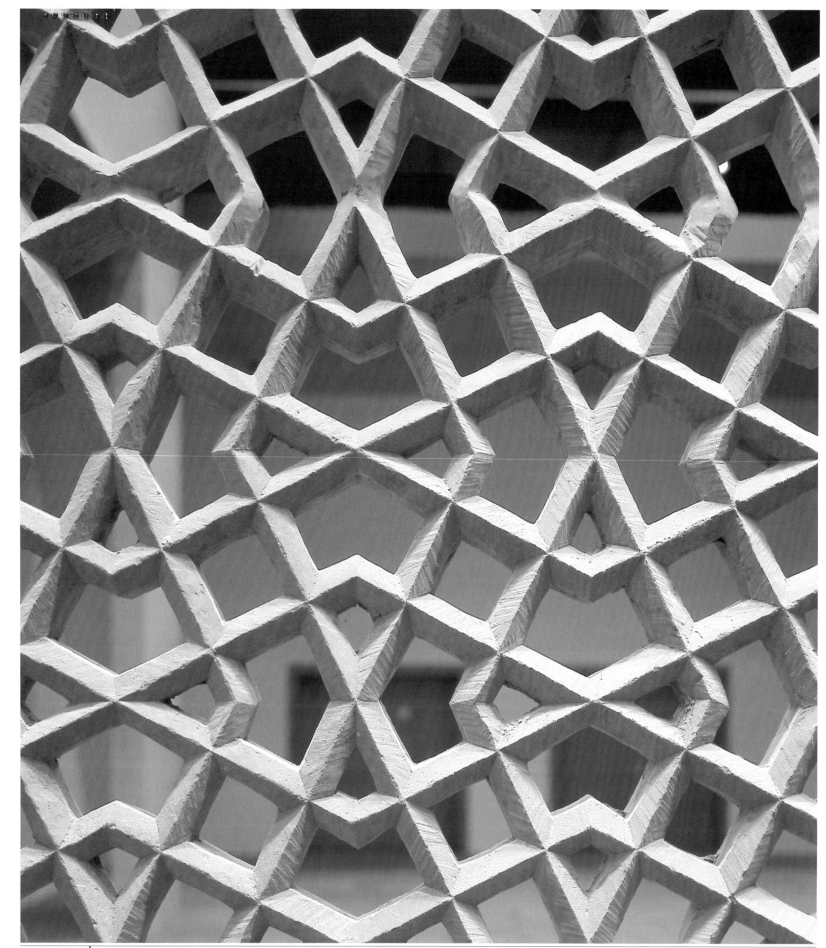

Léon Wohlhage Wernik Architekten
Indian Embassy Berlin, 2001
Stone lattice in metal frame

179 **Léon Wohlhage Wernik Architekten**
Indian Embassy Berlin, 2001
above: Entrance area
below left: Detail Grand Hall
below right: Partition

Renée Levi

Regina, 2000

Acrylic on wall of district heating power station
Regina-Kägi-Hof, Zürich-Oerlikon
Allgemeine Baugenossenschaft Zürich ABZ

Michael Lin
TFAM 08.09.2000–07.01.2001, 2000

Emulsion on wood
3600 x 1600 cm
View of installation Taipei Fine Arts Museum, Taipei
courtesy of Taipei Fine Arts Museum

183 | **Michael Lin**
Palais des Beaux Arts 06.12.03–22.02.04, 2003

Emulsion on wood
3200 x 2000 cm
View of installation Palais des Beaux Arts, Lille
courtesy of Lille 2004/Le Consortium, Dijon, Galerie Tanit, Munich

184

Michael Lin

Atrium Stadhuis The Hague, 2002

Emulsion on wood
5000 x 2500 cm
View of installation
courtesy of Stroom, The Hague

185 **Michael Lin**

In Sickness and in Health, 2004

Billboard
Contemporary Art Museum St. Louis, St. Louis
courtesy of Contemporary Art Museum St. Louis, St. Louis

186 **Michael Lin**
Three on the Bund, 2004

Emulsion on wood
1500 x 359 x 400 cm
View of installation Shanghai Gallery of Art, Shanghai
courtesy of Shanghai Gallery of Art, Shanghai

187

Michael Lin
Grind, 2004

Emulsion on wood
1600 x 650 x 390 cm
View of installation PS1 Contemporary Art Center, New York
courtesy of PS1 Contemporary Art Center, New York

188   **Daniele Marques**
Local Government Offices, Work Shops and Depot of the
Fire Brigade Münsterlingen, 2004
Coloured concrete with planking structure
Exterior view

Daniele Marques
Local Government Offices, Work Shops and Depot of the
Fire Brigade Münsterlingen, 2004
above: Concrete facade
below: Detail of facade

Agnes Martin

The Peach, 1964

Oil and graphite on canvas
183 x 183 cm
Dia Art Foundation, New York
Promised gift of Louise and Leonard Riggio
copyright Agnes Martin, courtesy of PaceWildenstein, New York

191 **Agnes Martin**
Earth, 1959
Oil on canvas
126,4 x 126,4 cm
Dia Art Foundation, New York
Anonymous gift in memory of Kirk Varnedoe
courtesy of PaceWildenstein, New York

Thomas Mass
ohne Titel (Guggenheim-Spirale) [Untitled, Guggenheim spiral],
2003
Acrylic on plastered wall
Work on wall at the Rotunda of the Künstlerverein Malkasten, Düsseldorf

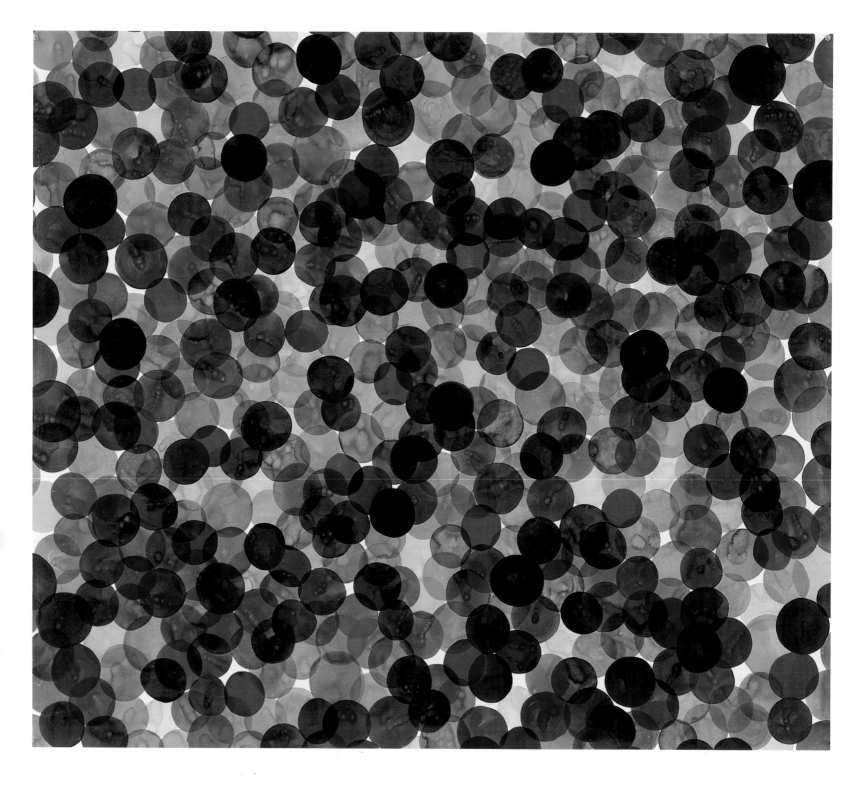

Thomas Mass
ohne Titel [Untitled], 2003
Ink on canson
130 x 152 cm

195 | **Thomas Mass**
ohne Titel [Untitled], 2004
Marker pen on canvas
40 x 30 cm

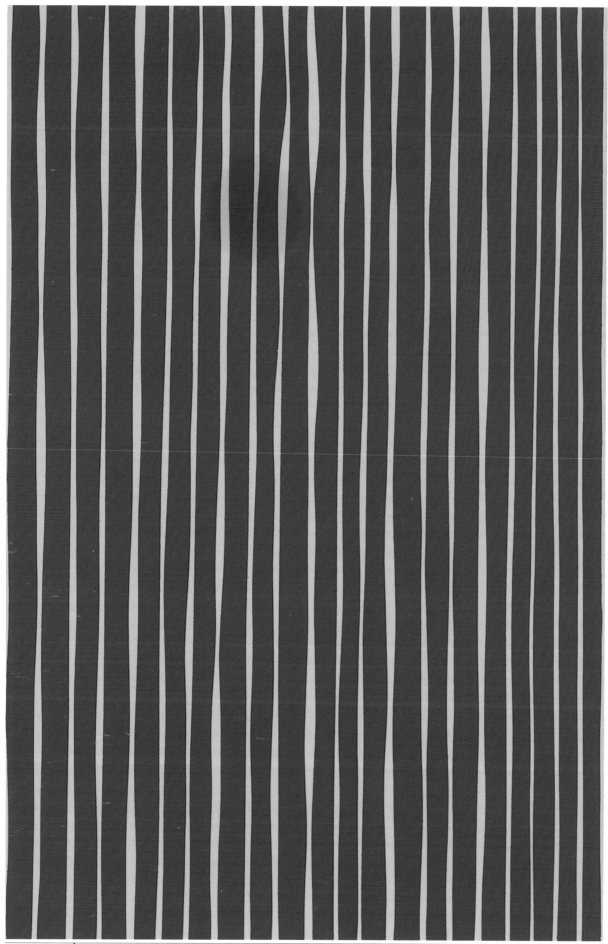

Thomas Mass
ohne Titel [Untitled], 2005
Oil, acrylic on cloth
90 x 60 cm

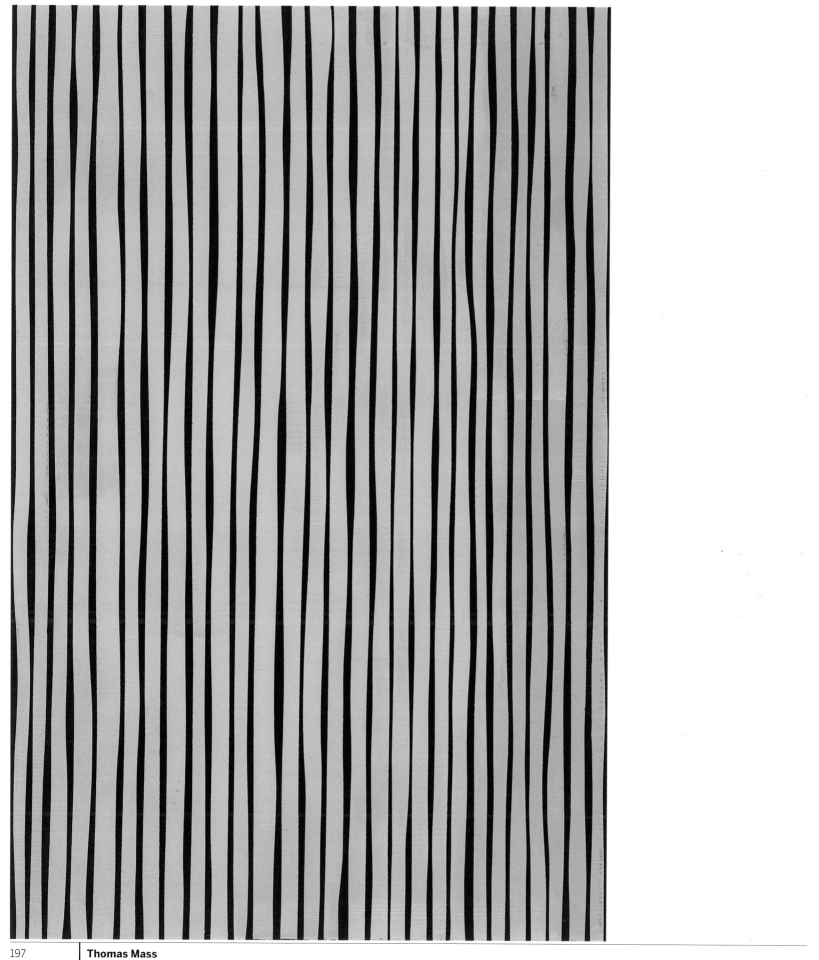

197 **Thomas Mass**

ohne Titel [Untitled], 2005

Oil, acrylic on cloth
90 x 60 cm

198 **Bruce Mau**
Skylight Graphics Art Center, 2004
Cushion made of fluoric synthetic foil
Study for Daly Genik Architects
Art Center College of Design, Pasadena

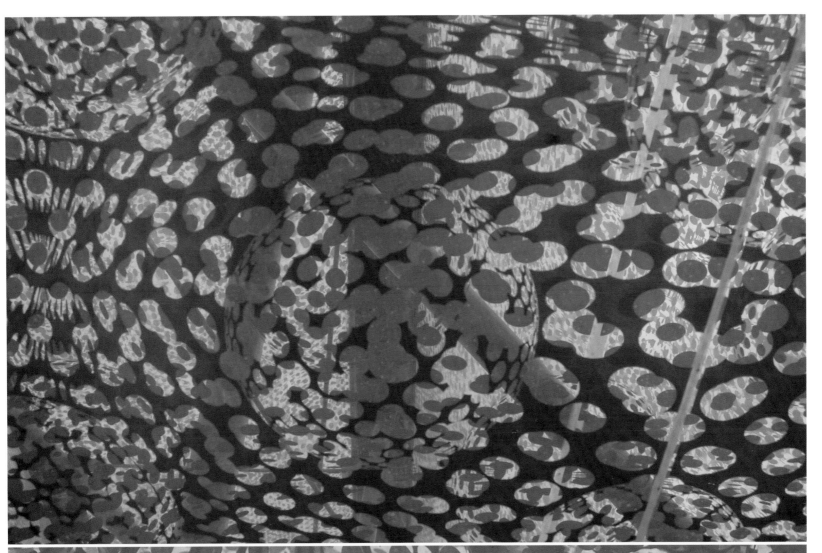

Bruce Mau
Skylight Graphics Art Center, 2004 (Details)
Cushion made of fluoric synthetic foil
Study for Daly Genik Architects
Art Center College of Design, Pasadena

Bruce Mau
MegaNano, 2003
Polyester
Manufacturer: Maharam

202

Paul Moss

Danger Painting 1, 2003 (Details)

Non adhesive tape on timber frame
246 x 196 cm

203

Paul Moss
Danger Painting 1, 2003
Non adhesive tape on timber frame
246 x 196 cm

204 **Markus Moström**
Blur, 2005
Inkjet print on cotton
Manufacturer: Sfera

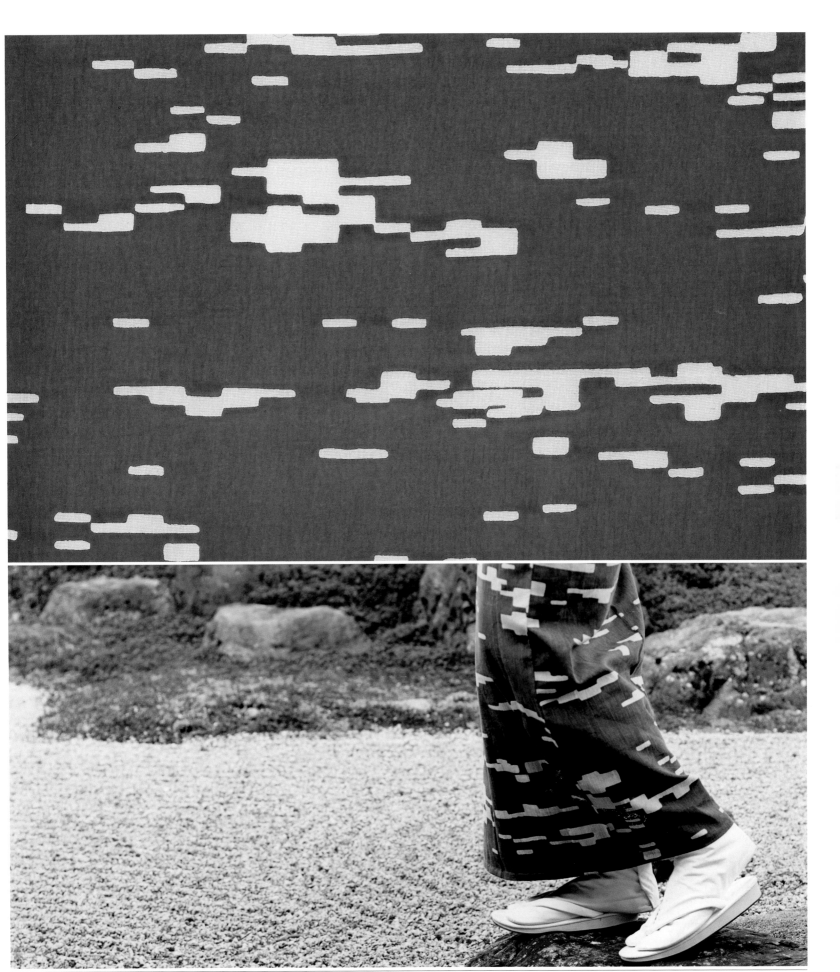

205 **Markus Moström**
Gleam, 2005
Screen-print on cotton
Manufacturer: Sfera

Markus Moström
Digit, 2005
Screen-print on cotton
courtesy of Sfera Building, Kyoto

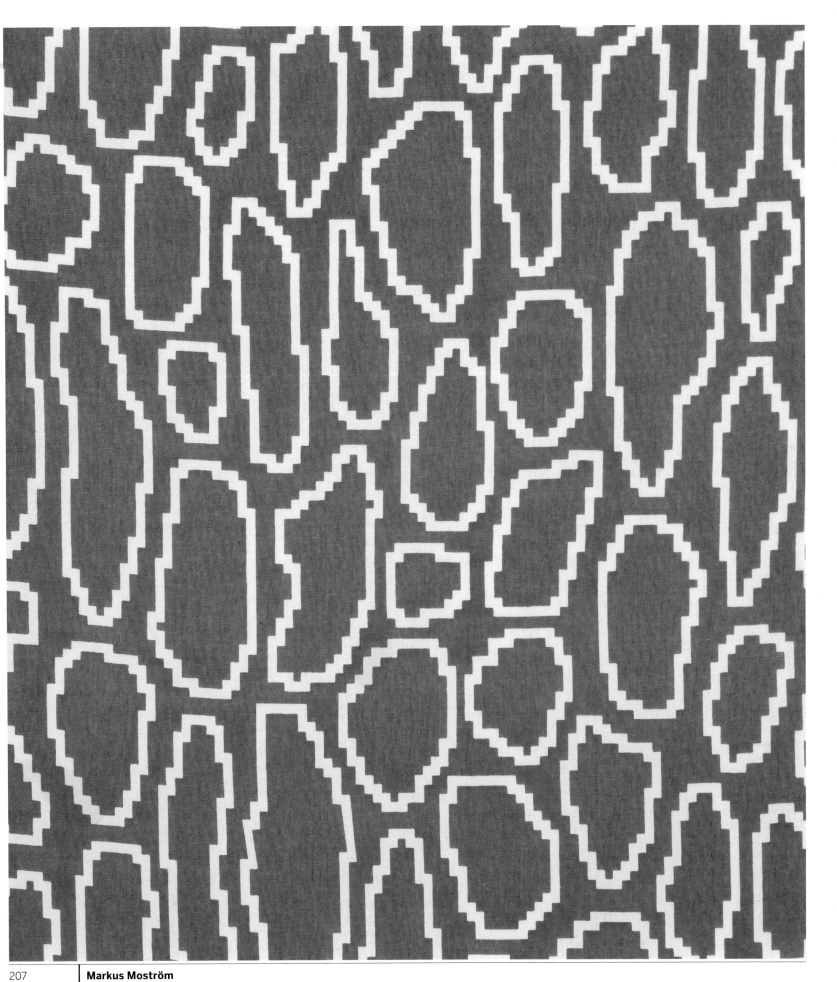

Markus Moström
Digit, 2005 (Detail)
Screen-print on cotton
courtesy of Sfera Building, Kyoto

Nägeli Architekten

Waldsiedlung Residential Development Berlin, 2004

Larch wood covering
above: Three single family homes
below: Exterior view

Nägeli Architekten
Waldsiedlung Residential Development Berlin, 2004
Entrance areas

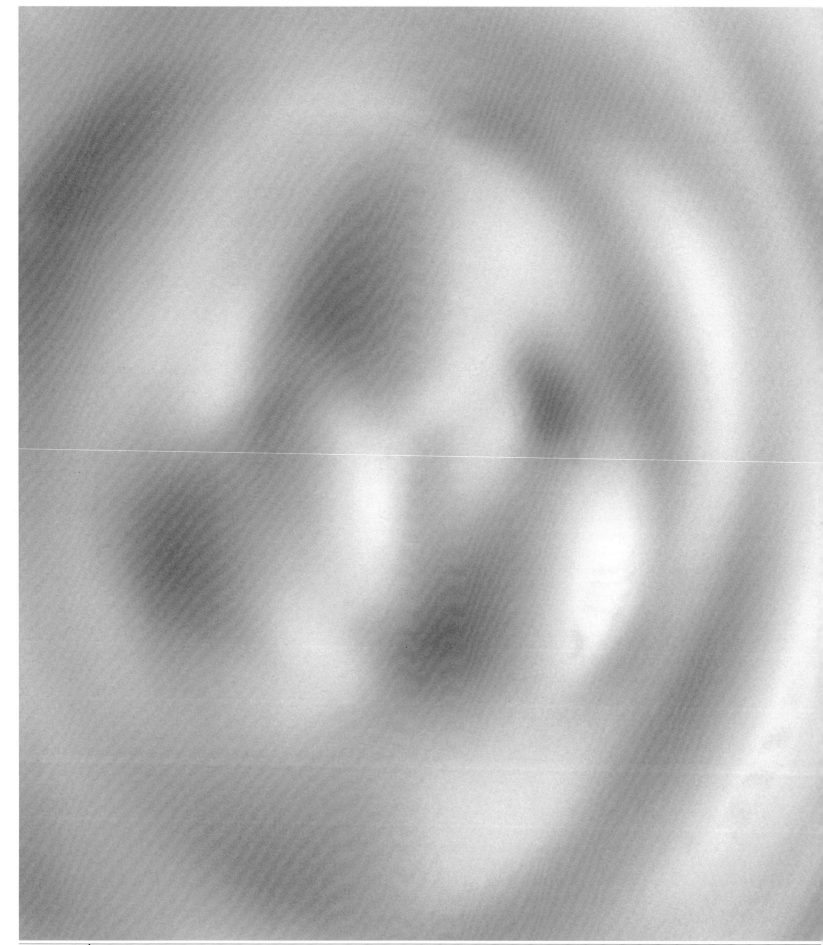

210 **Carsten Nicolai**

milch 10 Hz [milk 10 hertz] , 2005

Lambda print behind plexiglass
Series of 10 works, 80 x 66 cm each
Edition 5
courtesy of Galerie EIGEN + Art, Leipzig/Berlin

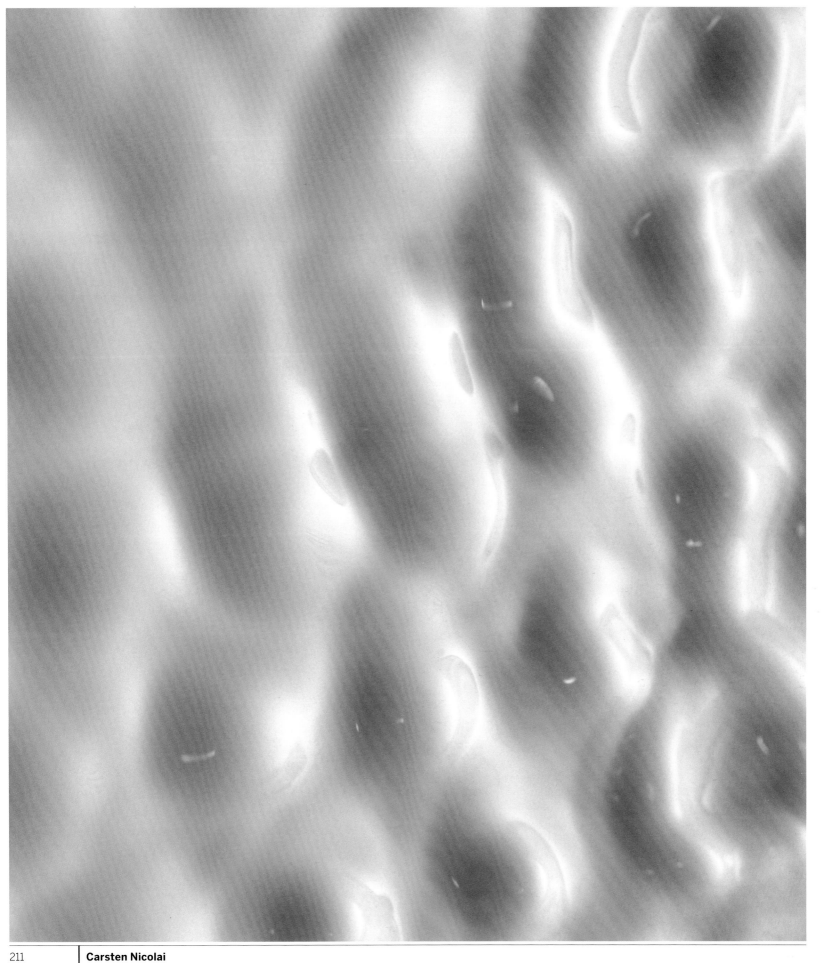

211

Carsten Nicolai

milch 25 Hz [milk 25 hertz] , 2005

Lambda print behind plexiglass
Series of 10 works, 80 x 66 cm each
Edition 5
courtesy of Galerie EIGEN + Art, Leipzig/Berlin

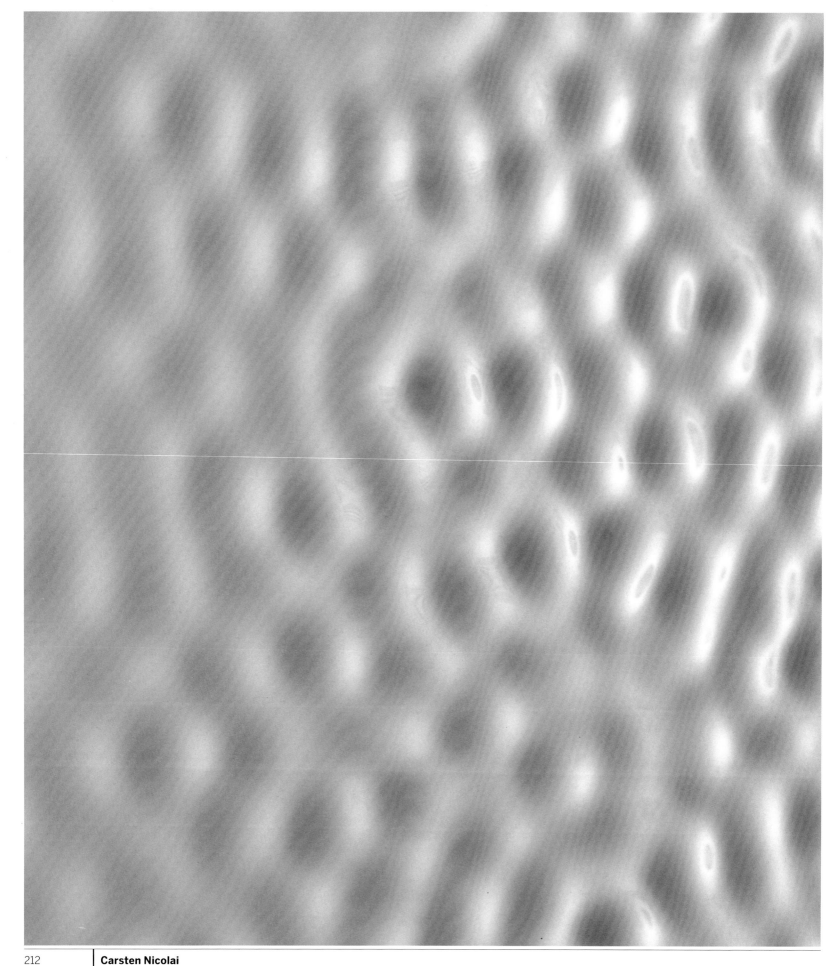

Carsten Nicolai

milch 55 Hz [milk 55 hertz] , 2005

Lambda print behind plexiglass
Series of 10 works, 80 x 66 cm each
Edition 5
courtesy of Galerie EIGEN + Art, Leipzig/Berlin

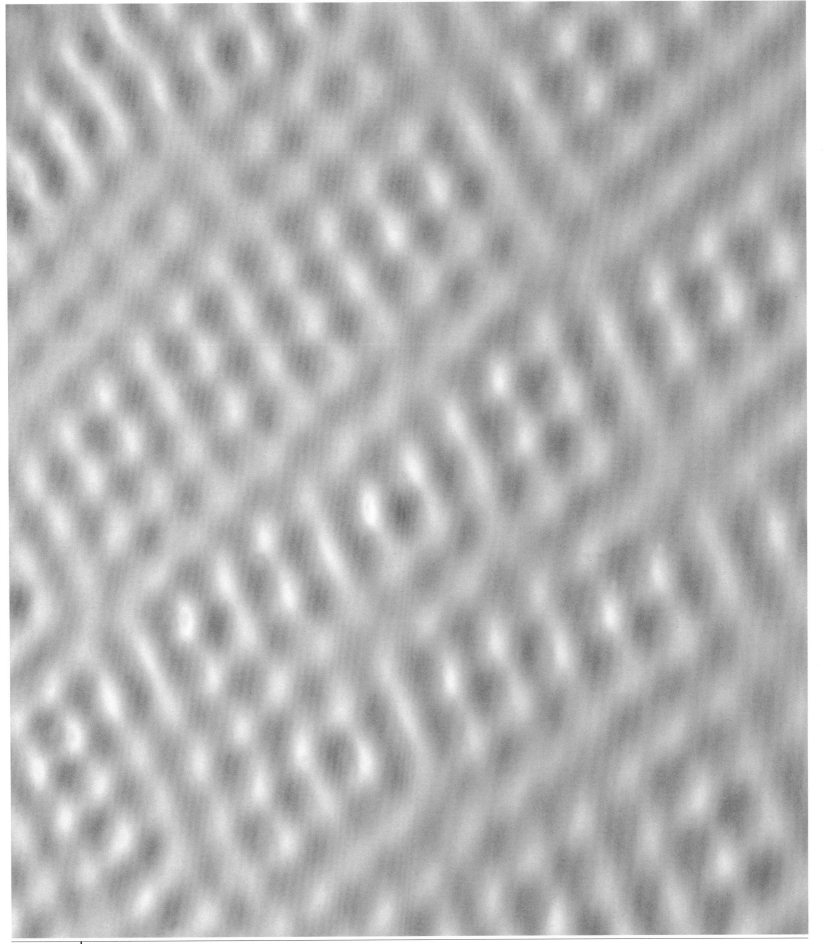

213 **Carsten Nicolai**
milch 95 Hz [milk 95 hertz] , 2005
Lambda print behind plexiglass
Series of 10 works, 80 x 66 cm each
Edition 5
courtesy of Galerie EIGEN + Art, Leipzig/Berlin

Olaf Nicolai
ohne Titel (Bluttropfen) [Untitled (drops of blood)], 2001
Posters, offset printing
100 x 70 cm each
View of installation Platea dell'Umanita Venice Biennial, 2001
courtesy of Galerie EIGEN + Art, Leipzig/Berlin

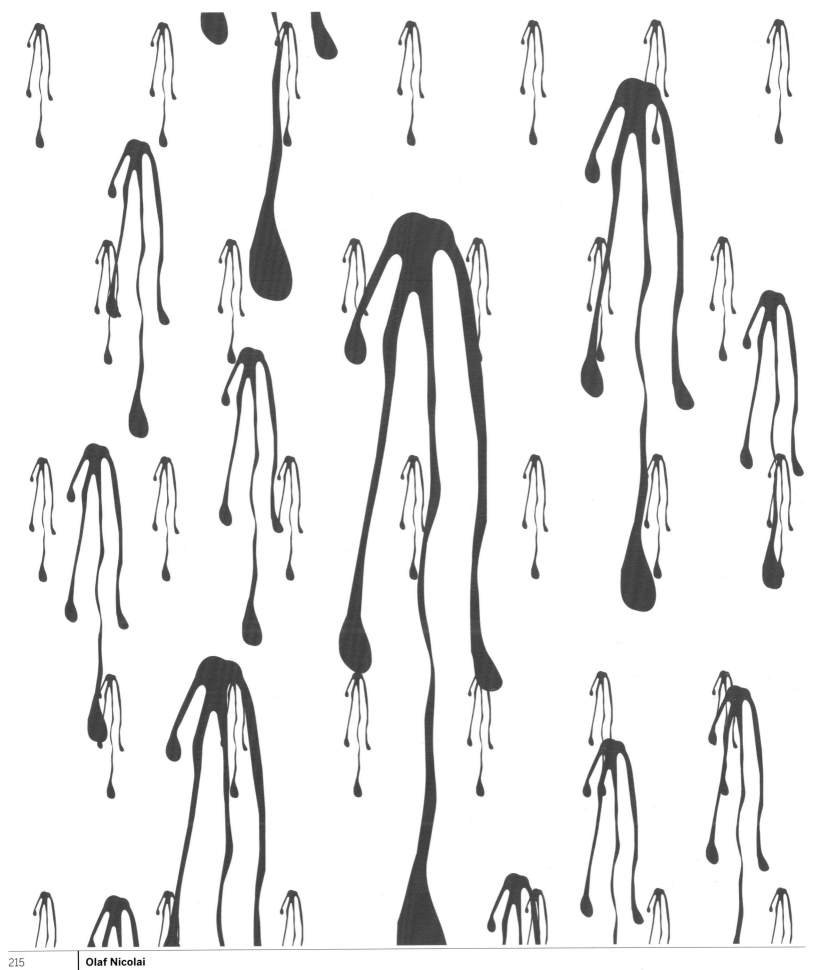

215   **Olaf Nicolai**
ohne Titel (Bluttropfen) [Untitled (drops of blood)], 2001 (Detail)
Posters, offset printing
100 x 70 cm each
View of installation Platea dell'Umanita Venice Biennial, 2001
courtesy of Galerie EIGEN + Art, Leipzig/Berlin

Olaf Nicolai

Camouflage, 2004

55,000 plants, dyed mulch
Sculptors' symposium Heidenheim 2004 with the support of the
Schiessle GmbH & Co.KG, Landscape Gardeners
courtesy of Galerie EIGEN + Art, Leipzig/Berlin

218 **Olaf Nicolai**
Module Dresden 68 (Photographic Study), 2000
Image source of the «rewind »forward coverdesign
Detail of facade

Olaf Nicolai
Cover Design for the «rewind »forward Catalogue, 2003
using the Module Dresden 68 motif
courtesy of Galerie EIGEN + ART, Leipzig/Berlin

Ateliers Jean Nouvel
Institut du Monde Arabe [Institute of the Arab World] Paris, 1987
Mechanism of blinds acting as sunscreen
Interior view

222 **Fabio Novembre**
UNA Hotel Vittoria Florence, 2003
Wood, glass tesserae
Interior view of the entrance hall
Manufacturer: Bisazza

Fabio Novembre
Bisazza Showroom New York, 2003
Glass tesserae
Interior view
Manufacturer: Bisazza

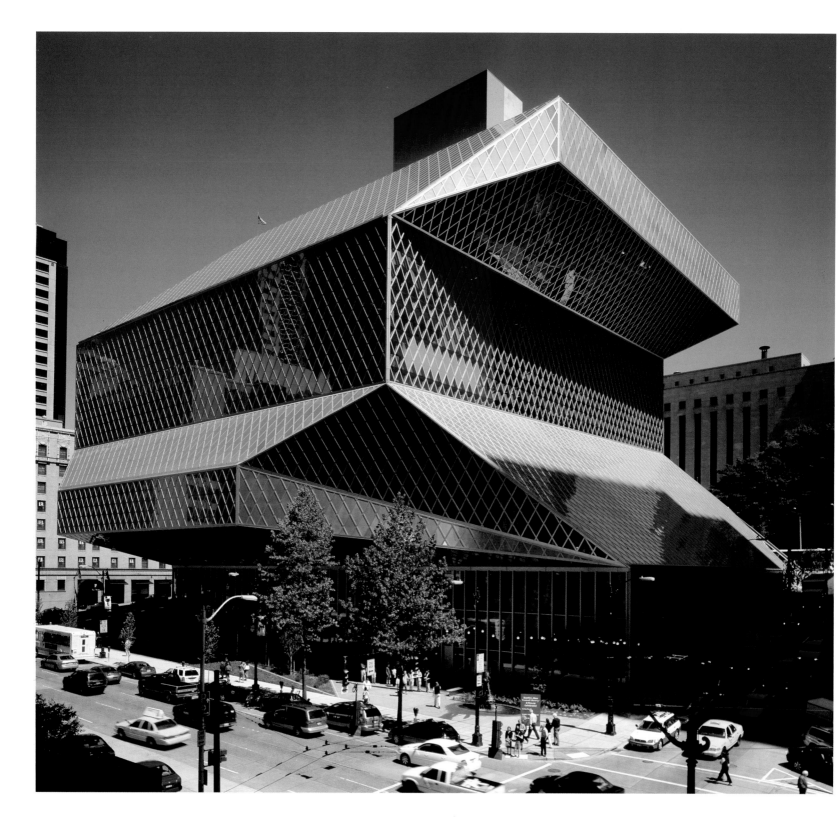

Office for Metropolitan Architecture
Public Library Seattle, 2004
Exterior view

Office for Metropolitan Architecture
Public Library Seattle, 2004
Interior view

Office for Metropolitan Architecture

McCormick-Tribune Campus Center, IIT Chicago, 2003

Pattern made of pictograms
above: View with subway station
below: Detail

Office for Metropolitan Architecture

McCormick-Tribune Campus Center, IIT Chicago, 2003
Portrait of Ludwig Mies van der Rohe made of pictograms
Study of 2x4 Studio, New York

230 **Susanne Paesler**
ohne Titel [Untitled], 2000
Gloss paint on aluminium
50 x 50 cm

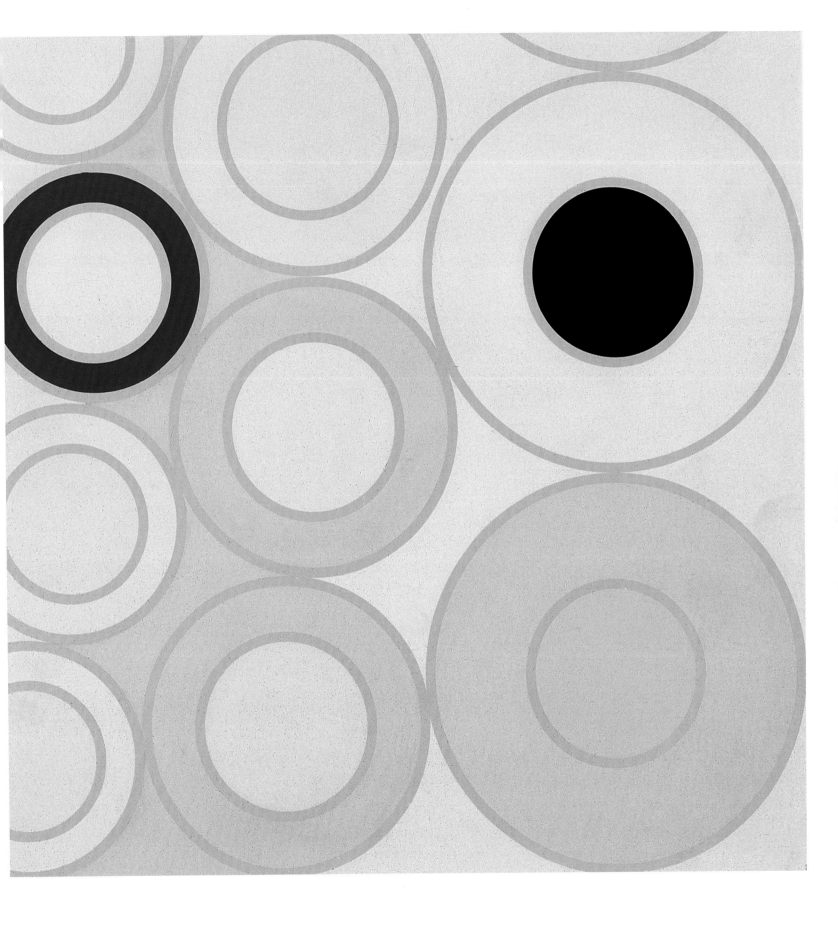

Susanne Paesler
ohne Titel [Untitled], 2001
Gloss paint on aluminium
180 x 180 cm

Susanne Paesler
Dark Flowers, 2005 (Detail)
Alkyd and gloss paint on aluminium
180 x 180 cm

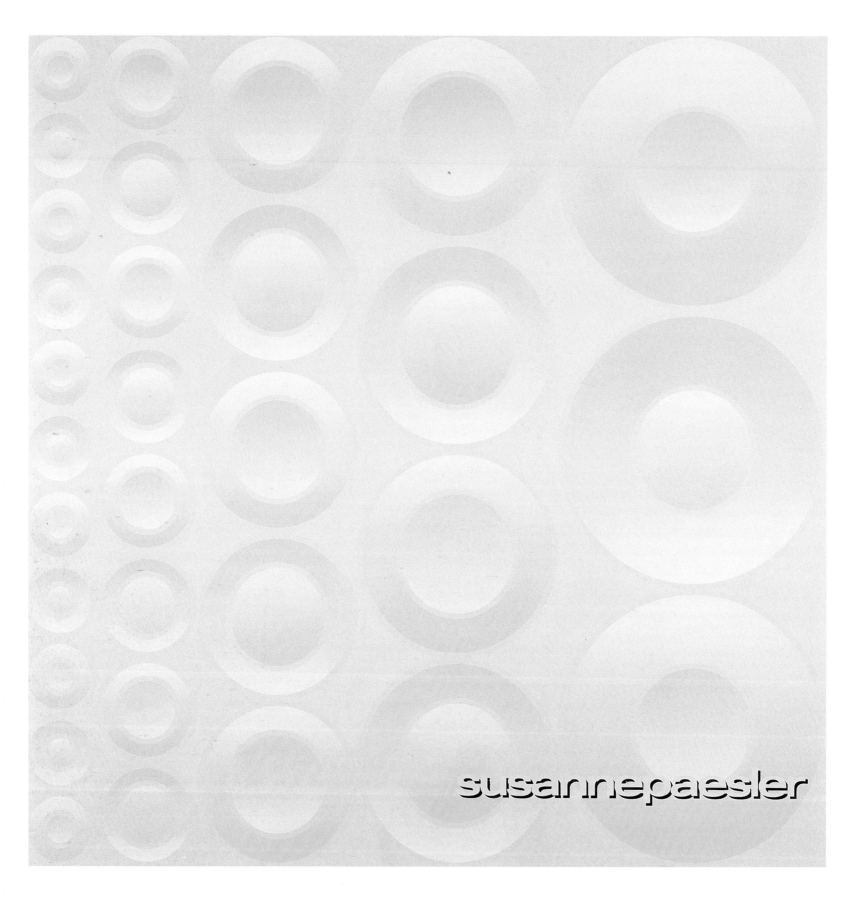

234

Susanne Paesler

Signature 1, 2001

Gloss paint on aluminium
180 x 180 cm

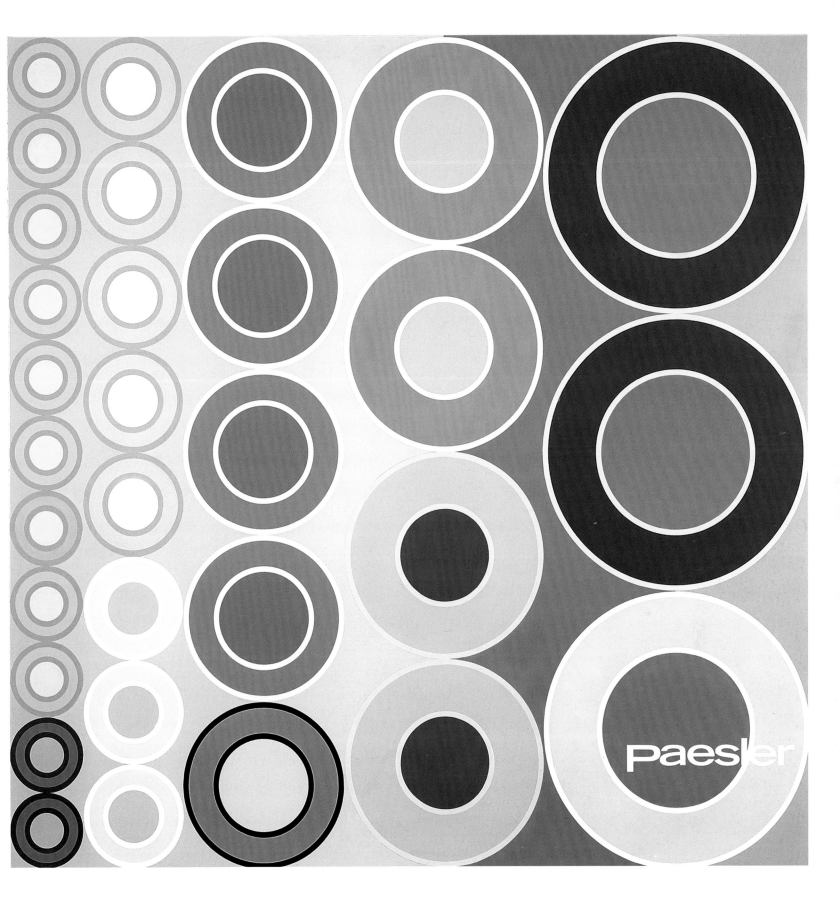

235

Susanne Paesler
Signature 2, 2002
Gloss paint on aluminium
180 x 180 cm

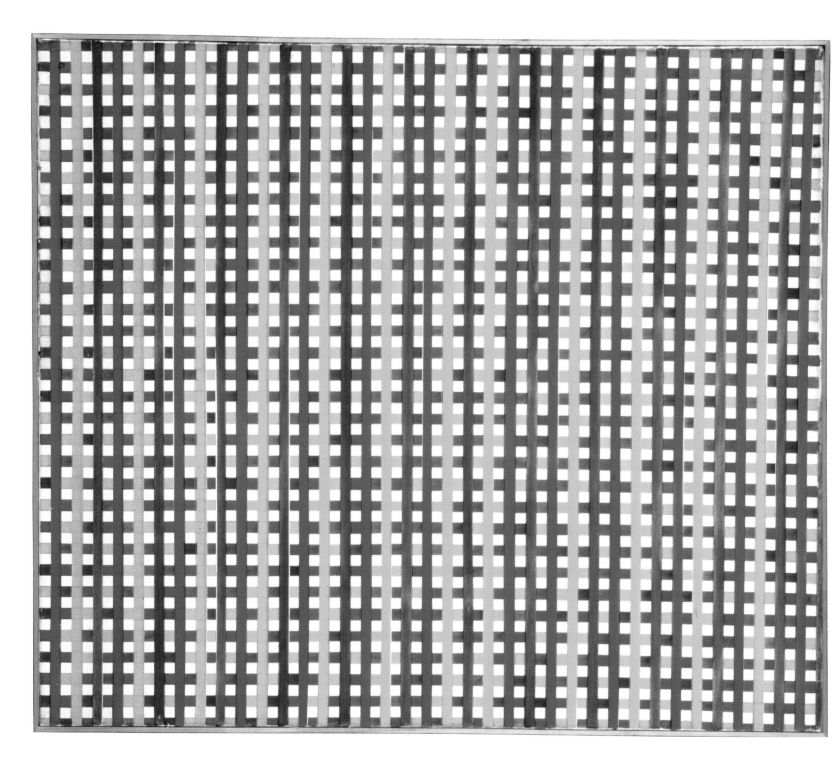

Blinky Palermo
Straight, 1965
Oil and pencil on canvas
80 x 95 cm
Pinakothek der Moderne, Munich

237 | **Blinky Palermo**
Flipper, 1965
Oil on canvas
89 x 69,5 cm
Pinakothek der Moderne, Munich

Architects Patterson
Stratis Residential Building Auckland, 2005
Concrete elements
West facade

Architects Patterson
Stratis Residential Building Auckland, 2005
Concrete elements
End wall with relief

Karim Rashid
Nooch Singapore, 2005
Travertine laminate, study of wallpaper for Wolf Gordon
Furniture by Karim Rashid for Frighetto and Magis

242 **Karim Rashid**
Nooch Singapore, 2005 (Details)
Travertine laminate, study of wallpaper for Wolf Gordon
Furniture by Karim Rashid for Frighetto and Magis

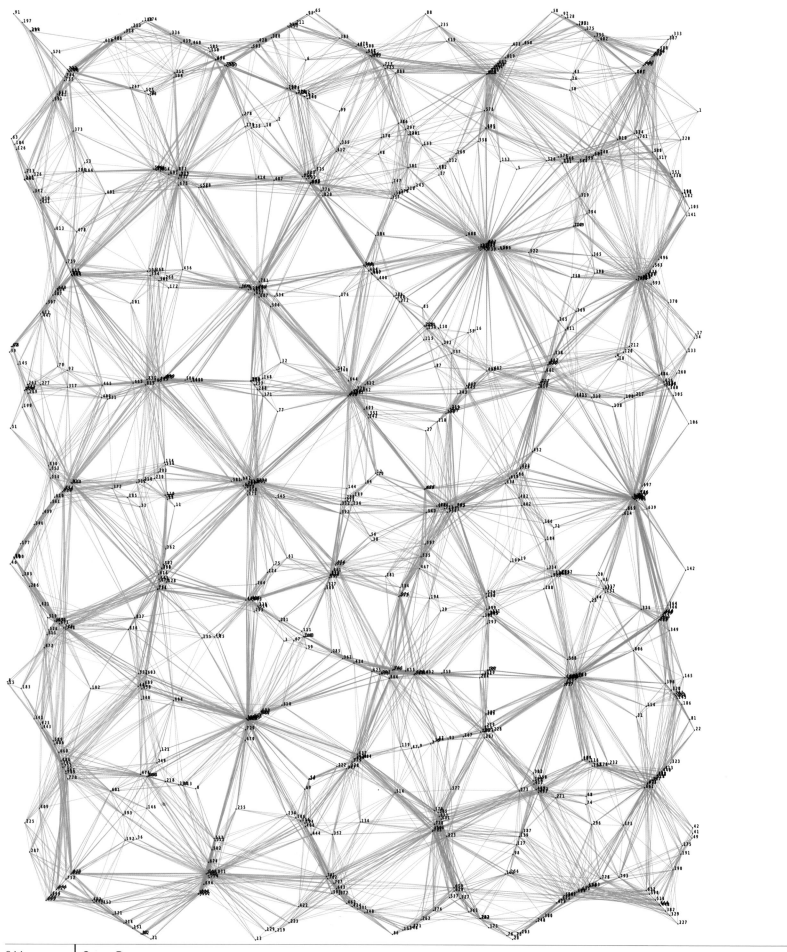

Casey Reas
Process 4 (Form 2), 2005
Inkjet print
36 x 28 cm

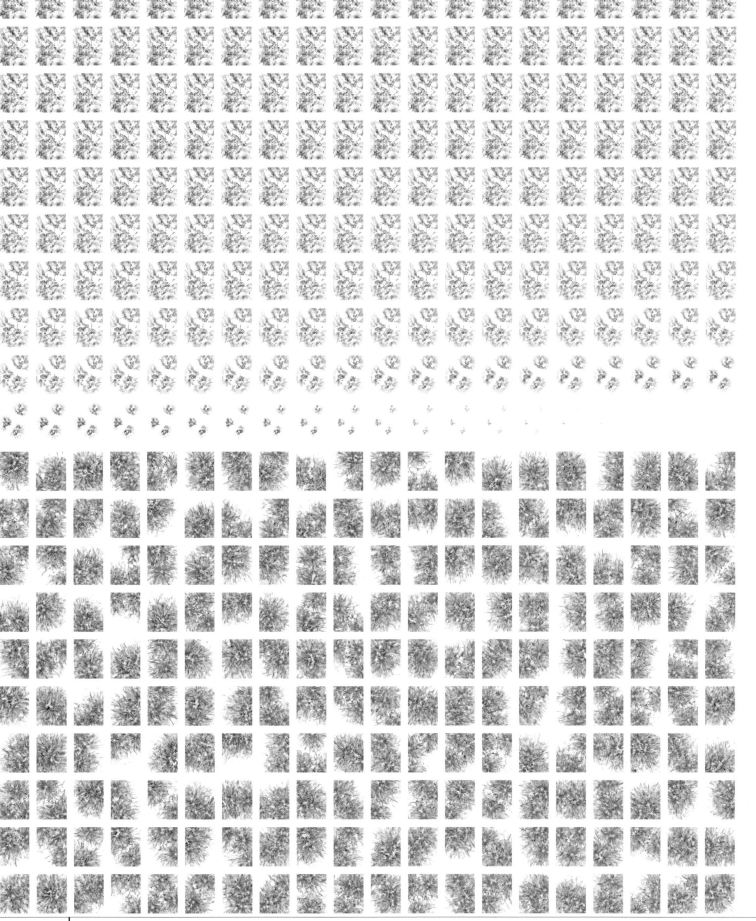

245 | **Casey Reas**
Process 6 (Image 1), 2005
Inkjet print
56 x 91 cm

below:
Process 6 (Image 2), 2005
Inkjet print
56 x 91 cm

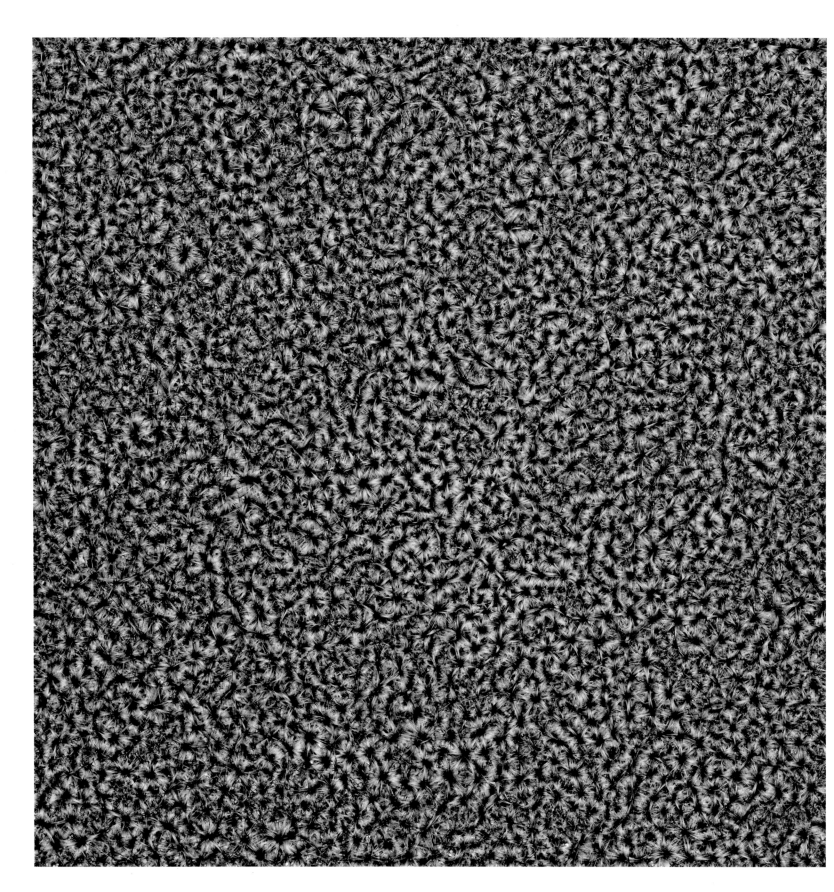

246

Casey Reas
Process 4 (Image 1), 2005
Inkjet print
73 x 73 cm

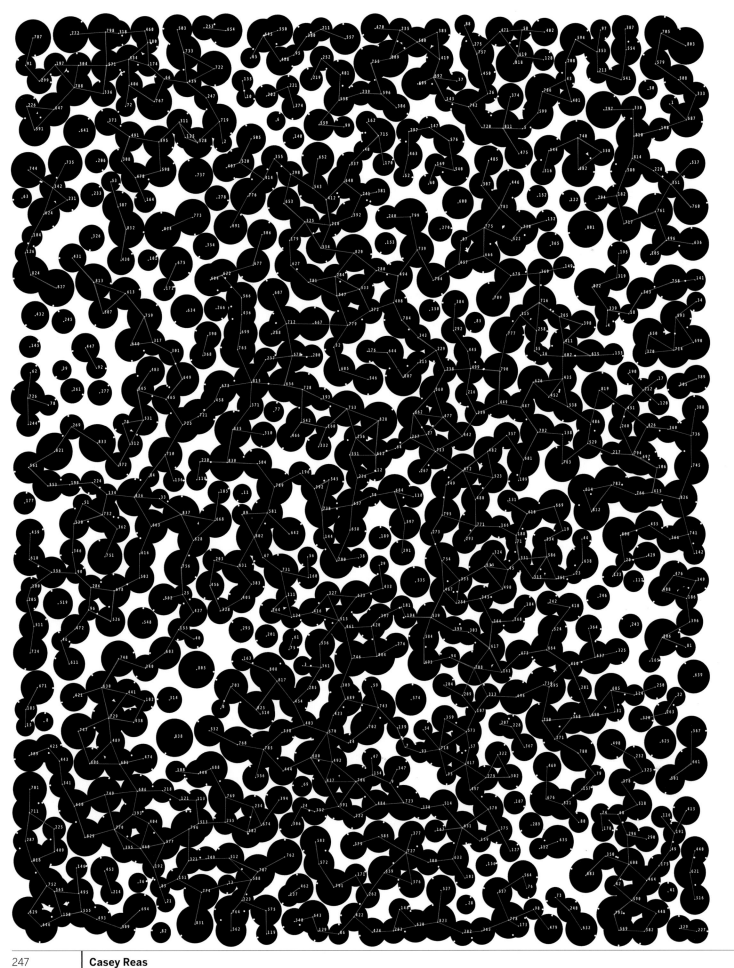

Casey Reas
Process 4 (Form 1), 2005
Inkjet print
36 x 28 cm

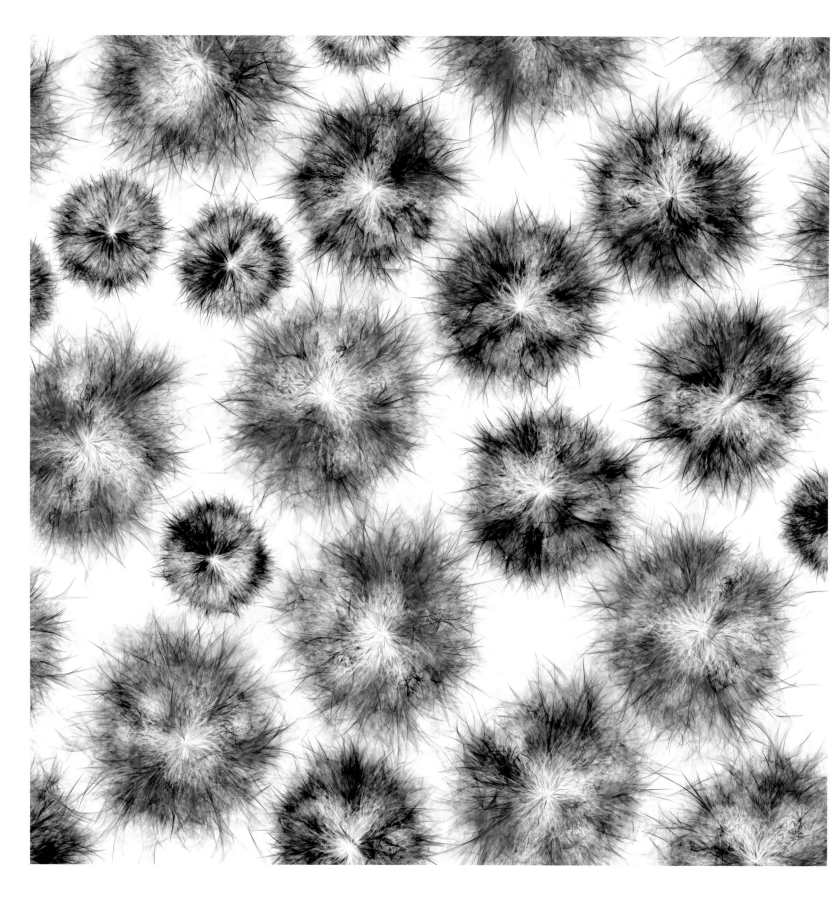

Casey Reas
Process 6 (Image 4), 2005
Inkjet print
73 x 73 cm

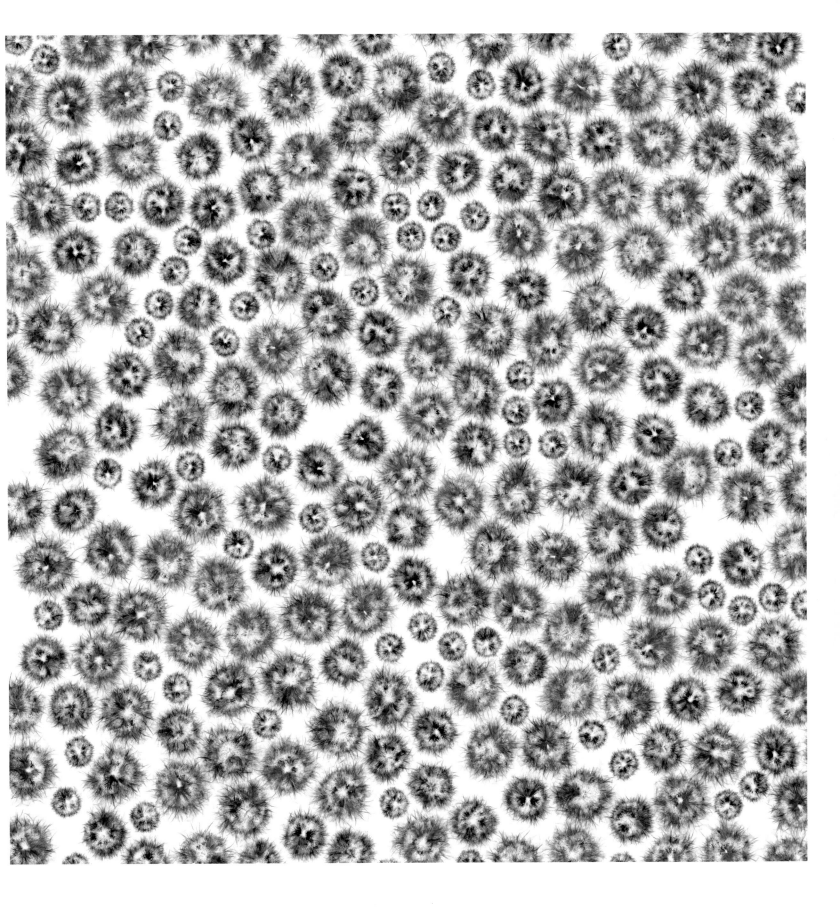

Casey Reas
Process 6 (Image 3), 2005
Inkjet print
73 x 73 cm

David Reed
531, 2004/05
Oil, alkyd on polyester
66 x 259 cm
courtesy of Galerie Bob van Orsouw, Zurich

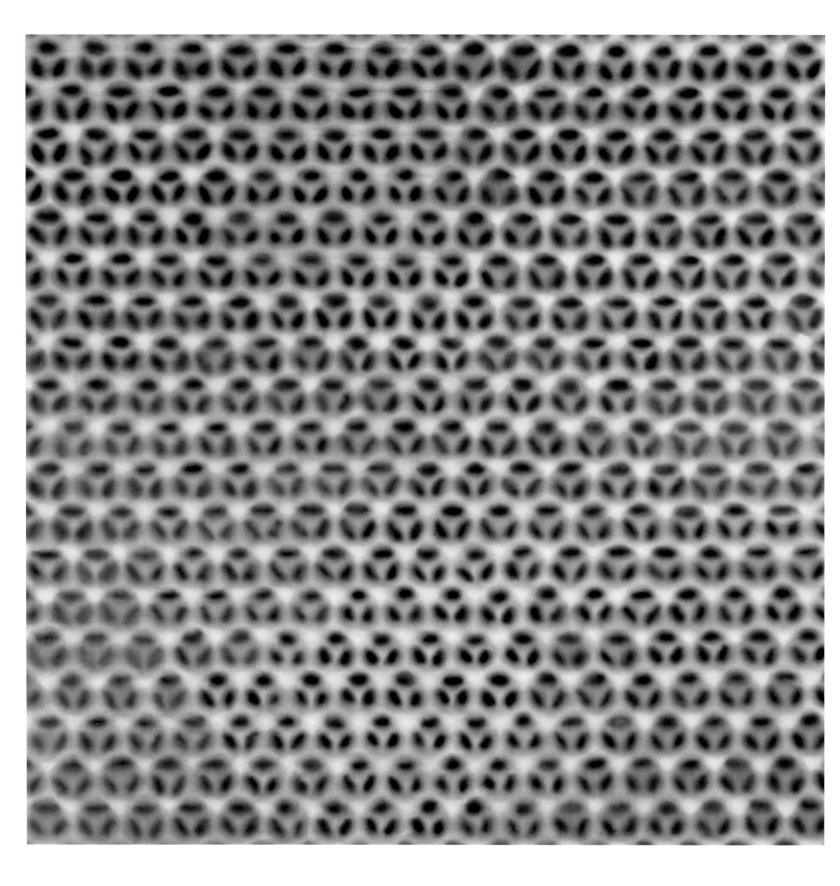

Gerhard Richter
Silikat, 2003 (885-1)
Oil on canvas
290 x 290 cm
Private collection

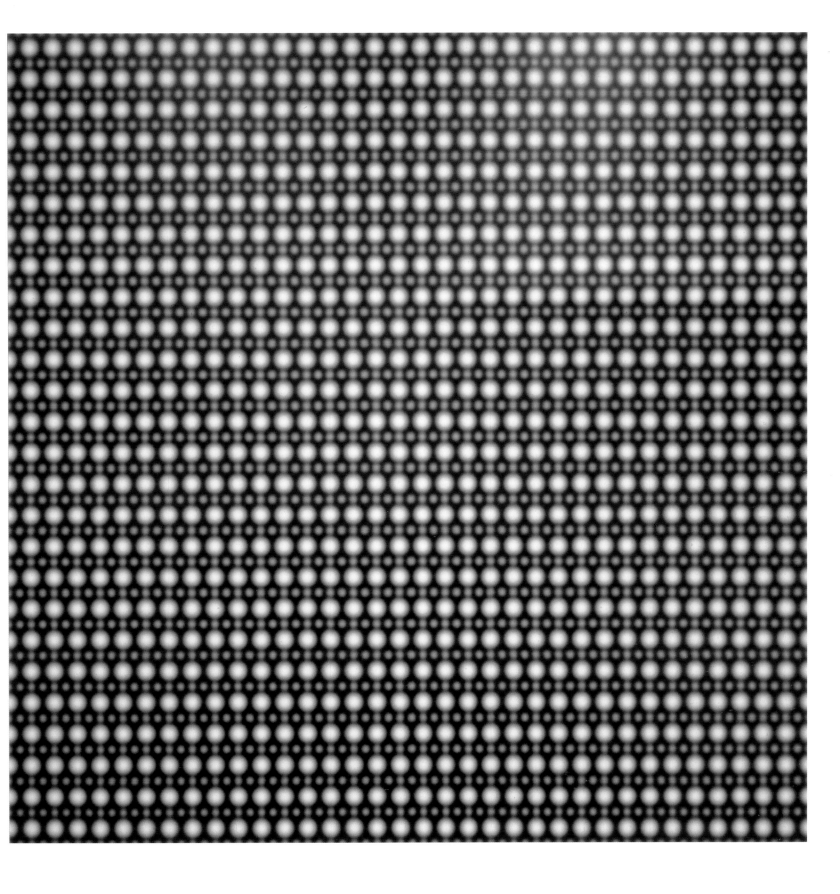

Gerhard Richter

Strontium, 2004 (888)

C-Print
130 parts, 910 x 945 cm
Fine Arts Museum of San Francisco

254 | **Bridget Riley**
Chant 2, 1967
Acrylic on canvas
231 x 229 cm
Neues Museum – Staatliches Museum für Kunst und Design in Nürnberg
On loan from private collection

Bridget Riley

High Sky 2, 1992

Oil on linen
165 x 228 cm
Neues Museum – Staatliches Museum für Kunst und Design in Nürnberg.
Gifted to the Museumsinitiative e.V. by Dr. Karl Gerhard Schmidt in 1992

Rinzen
+81 Calendar, 2004
+81 Magazine, Tokyo
Study

257 **Rinzen**
Paper and String, 2002
Digital for screen-printing for book end paper

Rinzen
Heliotrope, 2003
Poster design

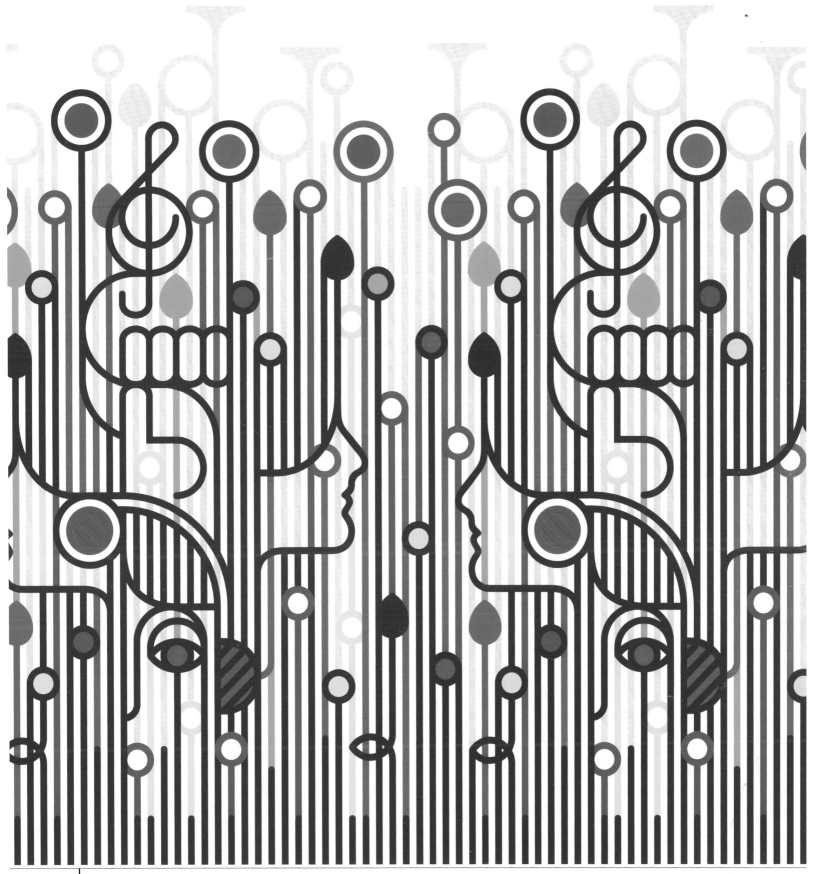

Rinzen
ARIA Awards, 2004
Posters, invitations and various print-materials
Corporate design for Australian Record Industry Association, Sydney

Rinzen
W+K Wallpaper, 2004
Study of wallpaper for the advertising agency
Wieden+Kennedy, Amsterdam

261

Rinzen

W+K Wallpaper, 2004

Study of wallpaper for the advertising agency
Wieden+Kennedy, Amsterdam

Peter Roehr
ohne Titel (TY-15) [Untitled (TY-15)], 1963
Typewriter on paper
18,9 x 19,3 on 32,2 x 29,7 cm
Museum für Moderne Kunst, Frankfurt/Main
Gifted by Paul Maenz, 1991

263 **Peter Roehr**
ohne Titel (TY-84) [Untitled (TY-84)], 1964
Typewriter on Paper
14,9 x 14,9 on 21 x 22,1 cm
Museum für Moderne Kunst, Frankfurt/Main

Sadar Vuga Arhitekti
Trnovski Residential Complex Ljubljana, 2004
Ceramic on aluminium elements
Entrance area

265 **Sadar Vuga Arhitekti**
Trnovski Residential Complex Ljubljana, 2004
above: Garden view
below: Street view

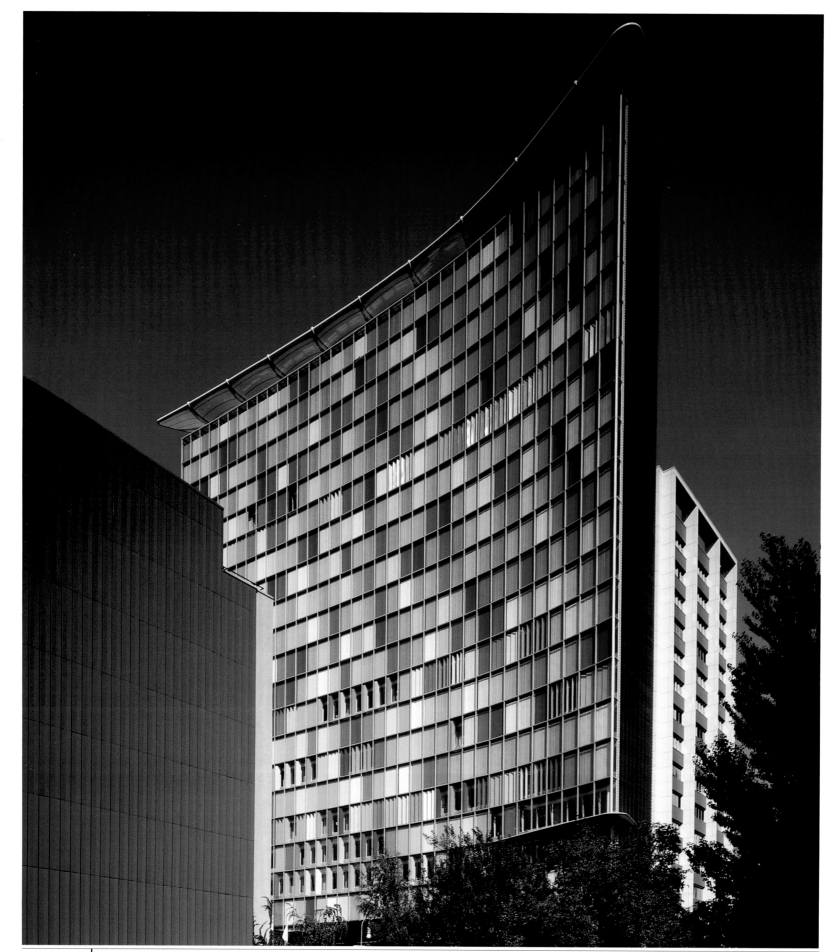

266

Sauerbruch Hutton Architekten

GSW High-rise Berlin, 1999

Vertical sunscreen slats
Exterior view

267 **Sauerbruch Hutton Architekten**

Photonics Centre Berlin, 1998

Coloured venetian blinds
above: Exterior view of testing plant (left) and of office wing and laboratories (right)
below: Interior view of testing plant

Sauerbruch Hutton Architekten
Laboratory and Office Building Biberach, 2002
Movable glass elements
Exterior view by day

Sauerbruch Hutton Architekten
Laboratory and Office Building Biberach, 2002
Exterior view by evening

Sauerbruch Hutton Architekten
High Bay Warehouse Dogern, 2002
Coloured metal panels
Exterior view

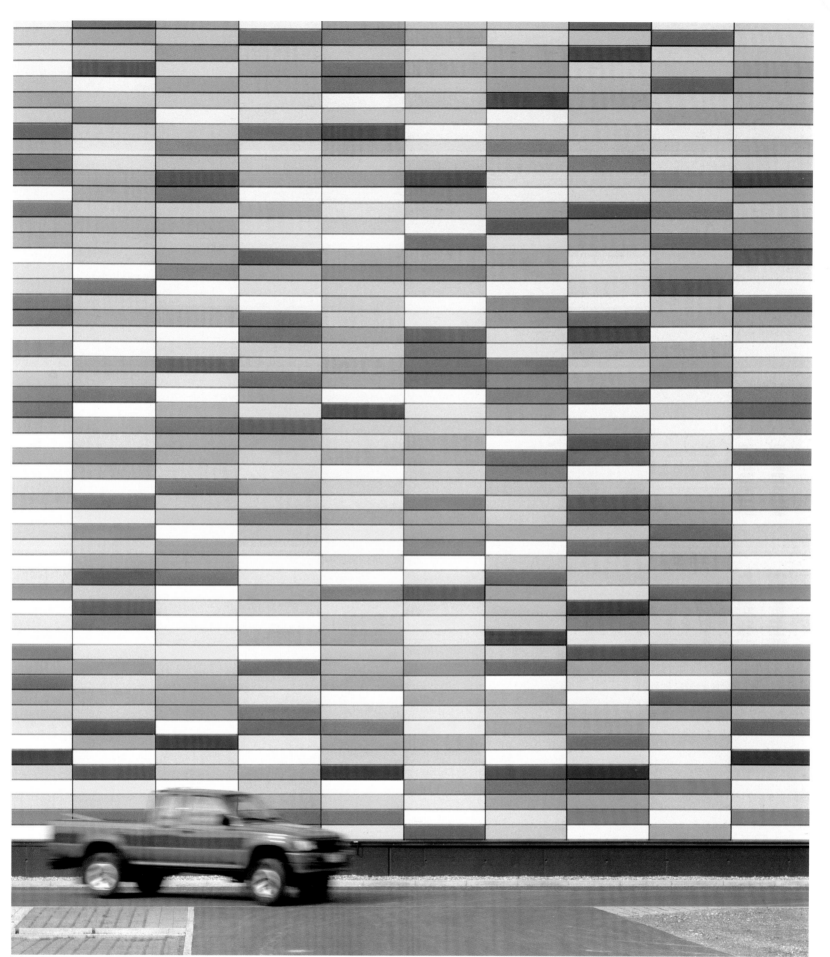

Sauerbruch Hutton Architekten
High Bay Warehouse Dogern, 2002
Coloured metal panels
Detail of facade

Paul Simmons
Euro Damask, 2004 (Detail)
Handprinted wallpaper, screen-print
Paul Simmons for Timorous Beasties

273 | **Paul Simmons**
Euro Damask, 2004
Handprinted wallpaper, screen-print
Paul Simmons for Timorous Beasties

Paul Simmons
Glasgow Toile, 2004
Wallpaper of hand printed linen, screen-print
Paul Simmons for Timorous Beasties

275 **Paul Simmons**

Glasgow Toile, 2004

Wallpaper of hand printed linen, screen-print
Paul Simmons for Timorous Beasties

Francis Soler

Ministry of Culture Paris, 2004
Stainless steel elements
View of old building

277 **Francis Soler**
Ministry of Culture Paris, 2004
Stainless steel elements
View of new building

Francis Soler
Ministry of Culture Paris, 2004
Stainless steel elements
Detail of fassade of new building

279 **Francis Soler**
Ministry of Culture Paris, 2004
above: View of old and new building from the street
below: Interior view of top floor offices

280 **Rudolf Stingel**
Home Depot, 2004 (Phase 1)
Room lining
Screen-print on Celotex TUFF – R
Dornbracht Installation Projects
View of installation Museum für Moderne Kunst,
Frankfurt/Main

left wall:

Sigmar Polke
Roter Fisch [Red Fish], 1992
Acrylic on printed canvas
303 x 403 x 5,5 cm
Museum für Moderne Kunst
Frankfurt/Main
Loan from private collection

right wall:

Rudolf Stingel
Ohne Titel [Untitled],
2004
Oil and gloss paint on canvas
3 parts, 280 x 194 cm each

Rudolf Stingel
Home Depot, 2004 (Phase 2)
Dornbracht Installation Projects
View of installation Museum für Moderne Kunst, Frankfurt/Main

Rudolf Stingel

Home Depot, 2004 (Phase 3)

Dornbracht Installation Projects
View of installation Museum für Moderne Kunst, Frankfurt/Main

Rudolf Stingel
Home Depot, 2004 (Phase 4)
Dornbracht Installation Projects
View of installation Museum für Moderne Kunst, Frankfurt/Main

284

Anisa Suthayalai
Holiday Card, 2002
Paper
Study for 2x4 Studio, Client: Vitra

Anisa Suthayalai
Herbarium Bag, 2003
Paper
Study for 2x4 Studio, Client: Vitra

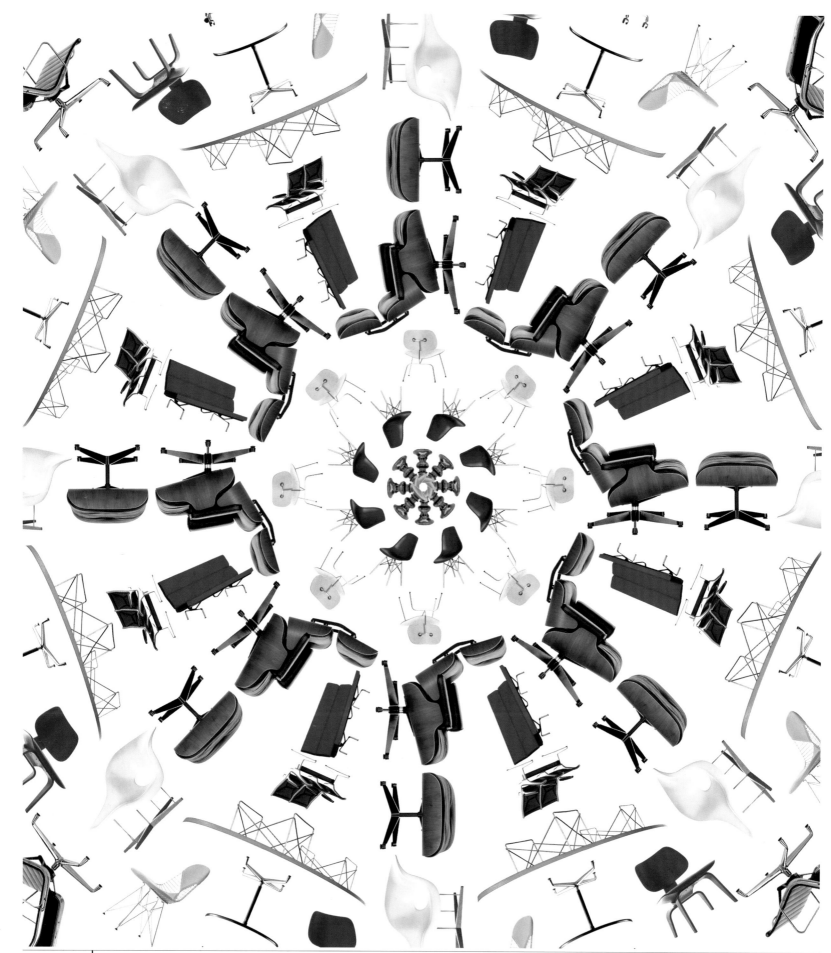

Anisa Suthayalai
Flower Pattern, 2003
Study for 2x4 Studio, Client: Vitra

Anisa Suthayalai
Nest, 2004
Study for 2x4 Studio, Client: Vitra

288 **Philip Taaffe**

Phasmidae, 2002

Mixed media on canvas
142 x 177 cm
courtesy of Jablonka Galerie, Cologne
Private collection

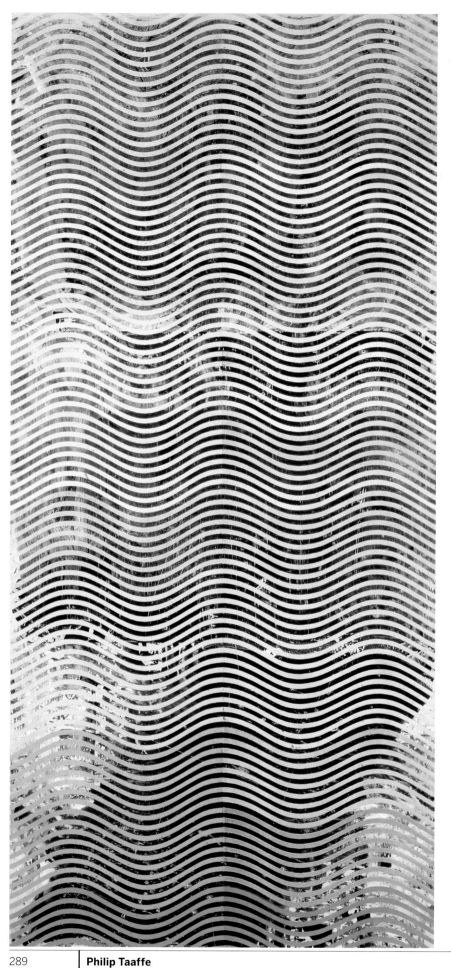

289 **Philip Taaffe**

Chasm, 2002

Mixed media on linen
213 x 100 cm
courtesy of Jablonka Galerie, Cologne
Private collection

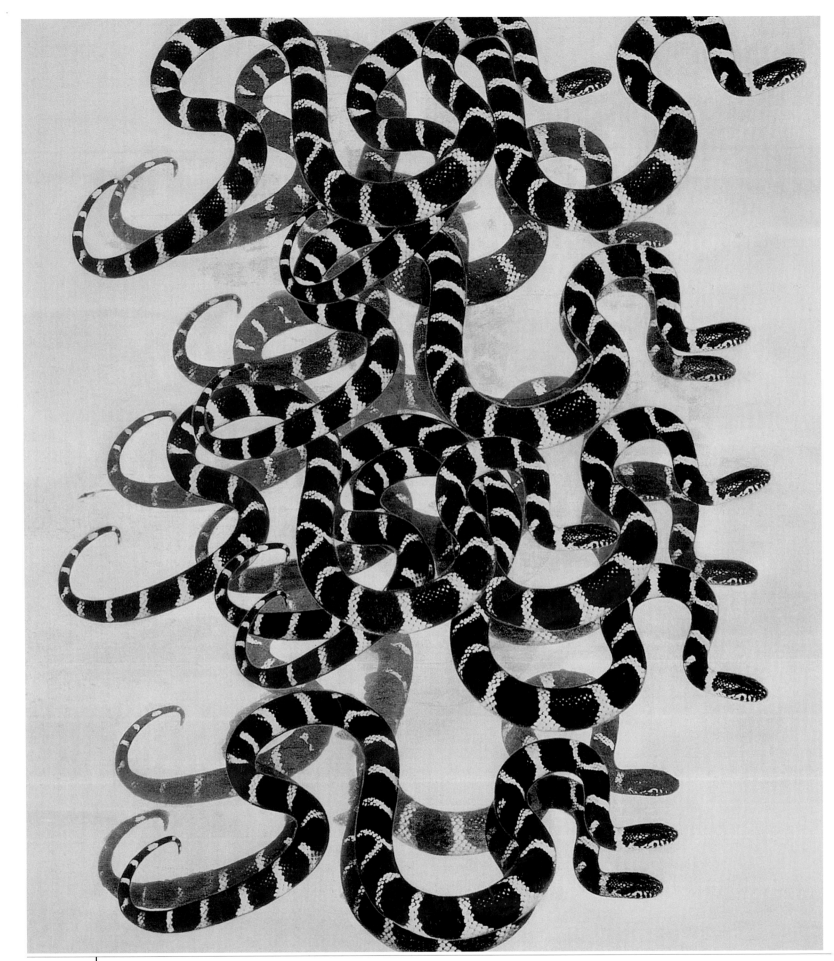

Philip Taaffe

Banded King Snake Counterpoise, 2004

Mixed media on canvas
2 parts, 115,8 x 94 cm each
courtesy of Jablonka Galerie, Cologne
Private collection

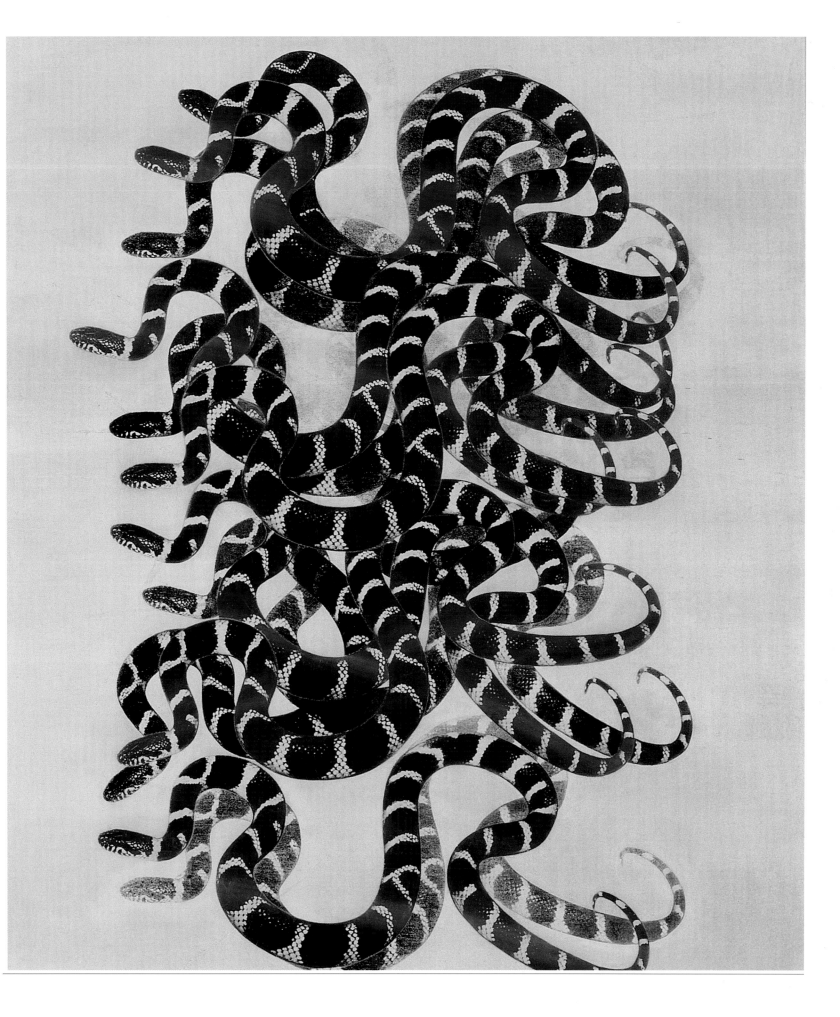

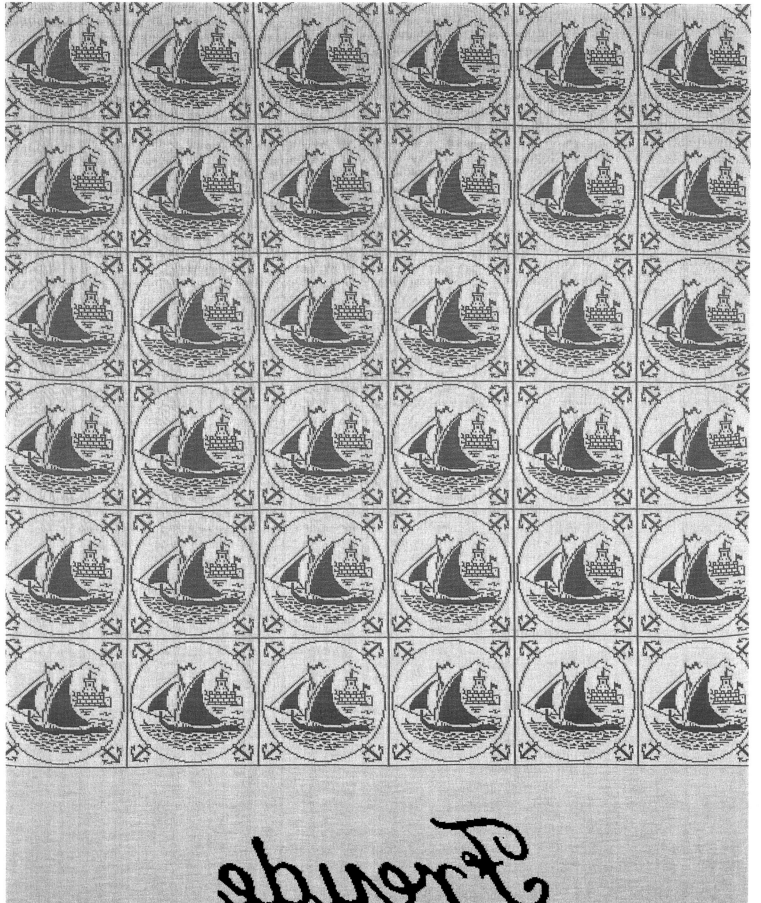

292 **Rosemarie Trockel**
Freude [Joy], 1988
Wool
210 x 175 cm
Neues Museum – Staatliches Museum für Kunst und Design in Nürnberg
Reiner Speck Collection, on loan from the City of Nuremberg

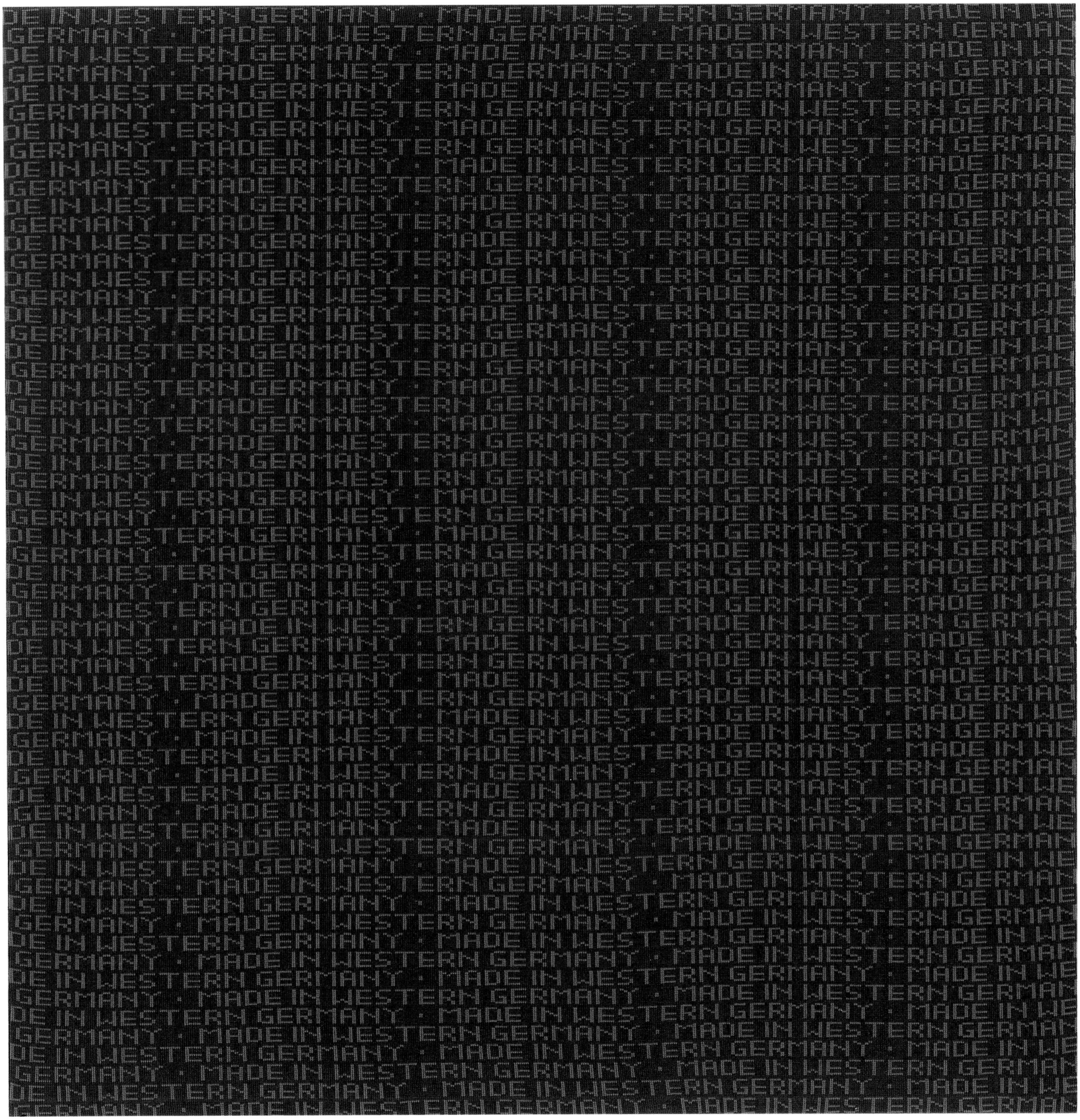

293 **Rosemarie Trockel**
Made in Western Germany, 1987
Wool
189 x 200 cm
Spiekermann Collection

Jochen Twelker

Die Exkursion [The Excursion], 1997/2000

Oil on canvas
9 parts, 290 x 1730 cm
View of installation Kunsthalle Göppingen, 2002

Jochen Twelker

Chinatown, 2004
Watercolour on paper
54 x 73 cm

Jochen Twelker
Die Malerin [The Painter], 2003
Watercolour on paper
72 x 54 cm

Jochen Twelker
Arabesque, 2004
Oil on canvas
155 x 200 cm

Jochen Twelker

The Fans, 2004

Oil on canvas
220 x 200 cm

300 | **Victor Vasarely**
Zèbres [Zebras], 1937
China ink on paper
56 x 60 cm
courtesy of Michèle C. Vasarely, Chicago

Victor Vasarely
Riu-Kiu-C, 1960
Acrylic on canvas
115 x 115 cm
courtesy of Michèle C. Vasarely, Chicago

302 **Marcel Wanders**
Crochet Table, 2001
Cotton, epoxy resin
Manufacturer: Moooi

Marcel Wanders

Flower Chair, 2001

Chrome plated steel
Manufacturer: Moooi

Marcel Wanders
Sauna House, 2004
Glass tesserae
Manufacturer: Bisazza

Marcel Wanders
Winter Flowers, 2004
Glass tesserae
Manufacturer: Bisazza

306   **Heinrich Weid**

Muschelpavillon I [Clamshell Pavilion I], 1994 (Details)

White coated aluminium, embossed
Slab size 40 x 50 cm
Kunstmuseum Düsseldorf im Ehrenhof

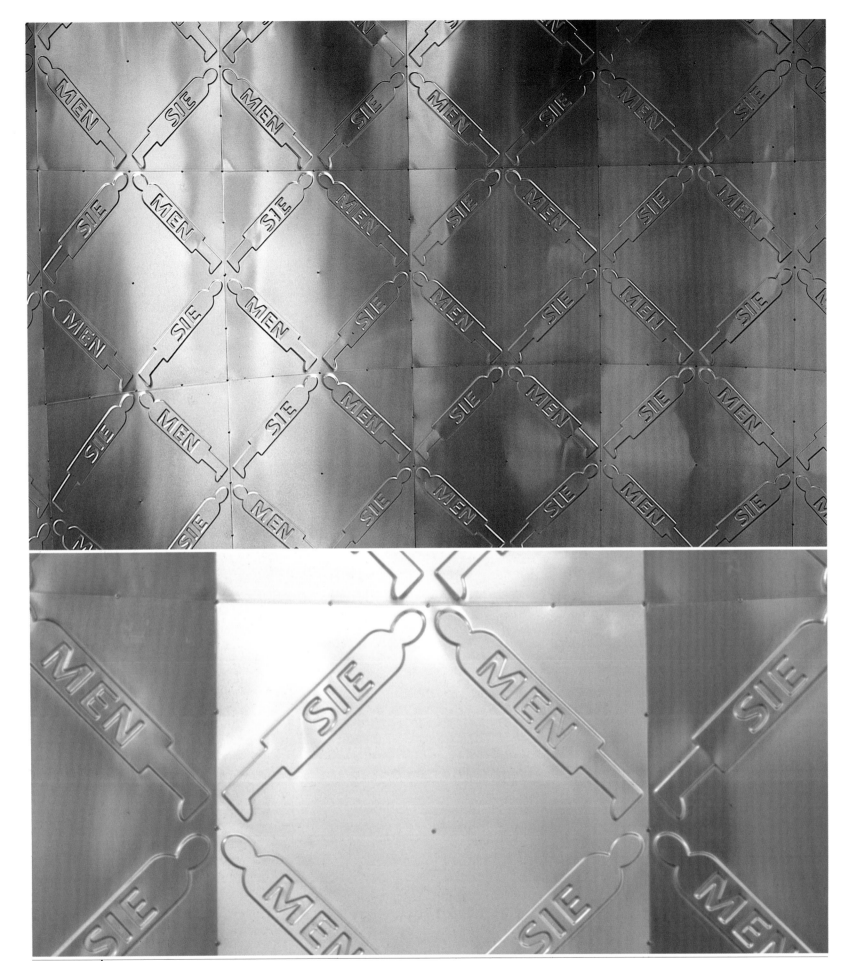

Heinrich Weid

Kreisender Pavillon für München [Rotating Pavilion for Munich],
1996 (Details)

Embossed aluminium sheeting on steel construction
Slab size 60 x 60 cm
Permanent installation: Richard-Strauss-Straße, Munich
Realisation: Büro Orange and Siemens Arts Program

Heinrich Weid

Kreisender Pavillon für Munich [Rotating Pavilion], 1996 (Details)

Steel rails with steel wheels and integrated electric engine, embossed aluminium
sheeting mounted on steel construction, with figures made of laser cut stainless steel
sheets, zinc sheets with stainless steel figures on lantern
390 x 290 x 290 cm
Exterior view of back wall
Permanent installation Richard-Strauss-Straße, Munich
Realisation: Büro Orange and Siemens Arts Program

Heinrich Weid
Wohnzimmer [Living Room], 2003
Knot-hole wallpaper, wood-effect earthenware crockery, table cloth
and seats made of tarpaulin with screen-printing
View of installation Kunstverein Alte Schule, Baruth

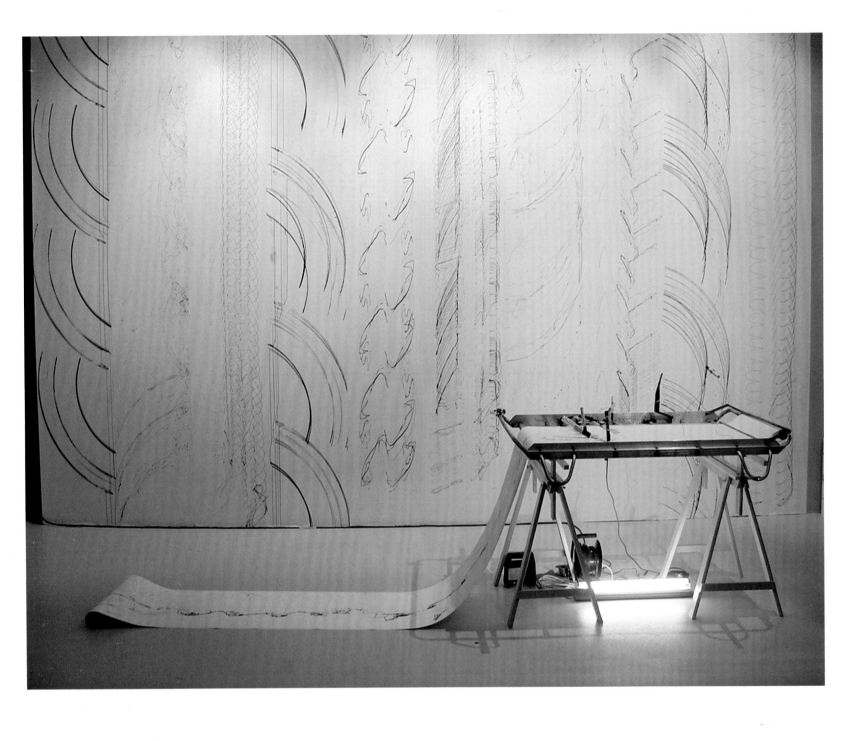

Hanna Werning/Joakim Ericson

Apparat No. 1 (Suddenly my wall was a mess – and I like it), 2005

Black permanent marker on white coated wallpaper
View of installation Färgfabriken, Stockholm

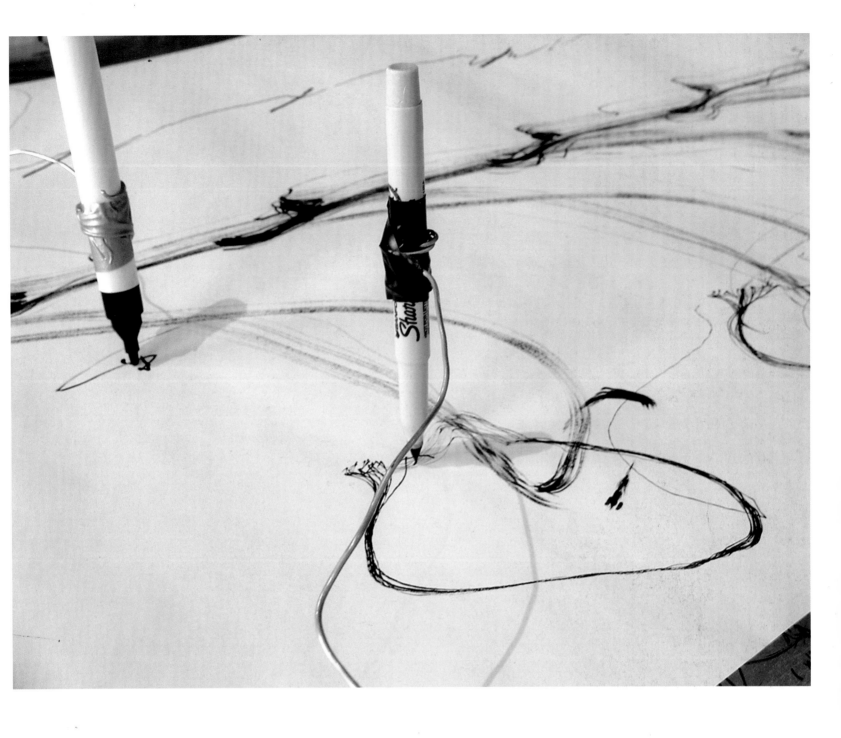

313 **Hanna Werning/Joakim Ericson**
Apparat No. 1 (Suddenly my wall was a mess – and I like it), 2005
(Detail)
Black permanent marker on white coated wallpaper

314

Hanna Werning
Krokodillöv, 2001–2004
Wallpaper/Poster, litho print
69 x 49 cm

Hanna Werning
Zebraskog, 2001–2004
Wallpaper/Poster, litho print
69 x 49 cm

316 **Ekrem Yalçindağ**
Schloss Balmoral 3 [Balmoral Castle 3], 2001–2002

Oil on canvas
80 x 80 cm
courtesy of Galerie Karl Pfefferle, Munich
Private collection

Ekrem Yalçindağ
ohne Titel [Untitled], 1996

Oil on canvas
45 x 35 cm
courtesy of Galerie Karl Pfefferle, Munich
Private collection, Frankfurt/Main

318

Douglas Young
Letterbox, 2002
Cotton print
Manufacturer: G.O.D.

Douglas Young
Yaumati Print, 2002
Cotton print
Manufacturer: G.O.D.

below:
Yaumati, 2002
Printed plastic
Hersteller: G.O.D.

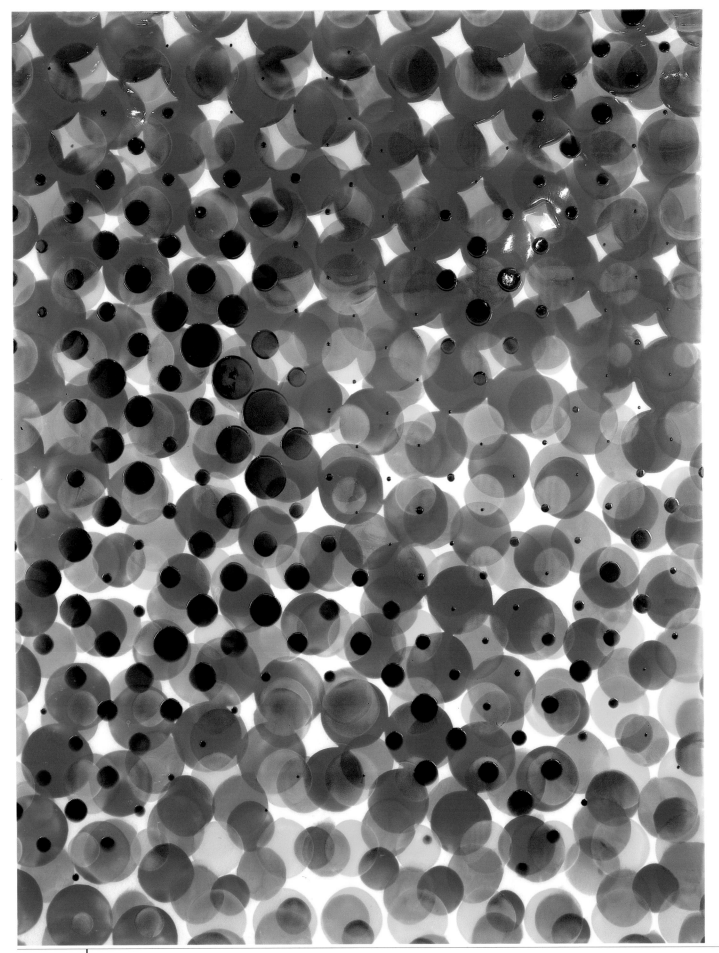

320 **Peter Zimmermann**

F-Raster, 1999

Epoxy resin on canvas
195 x 150 cm
courtesy of Galerie Michael Janssen, Cologne

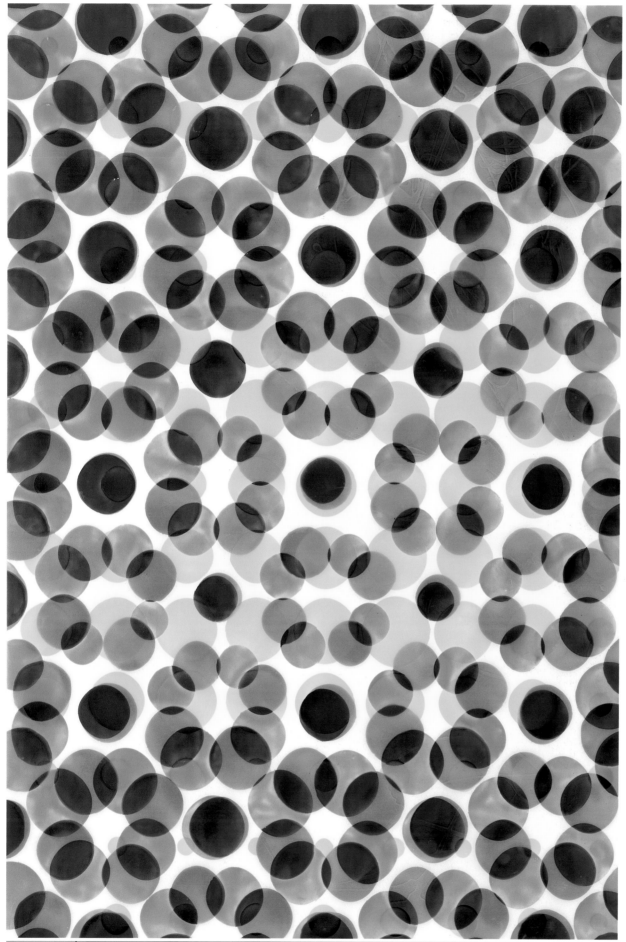

321 | **Peter Zimmermann**
L-Raster, 2003

Epoxy resin on canvas
200 x 130 cm
courtesy of Galerie Michael Janssen, Cologne

322

Peter Zimmermann
Scaffolding II, 2004

Epoxy resin on canvas
2 parts, 250 x 380 cm
courtesy of Galerie Michael Janssen, Cologne

A

Bettina Allamoda

Bettina Allamoda is an artist and lives in Berlin. She has undertaken teaching appointments at the University of the Arts in Berlin, among others. She works in various media like video, multivision and sculpture.

18/19 The facade of the Institute of the Arab World, which was opened in 1987 in Paris, is richly ornamented. The pattern is based on blinds, which adjust themselves via computer control to the prevailing light. The French architect Jean Nouvel introduced a new evaluation of ornamentation in architecture by combining an oriental language of forms with a high-tech aesthetic. The artist Bettina Allamoda is reflecting the new relationship between function and form, between surface and construction, in the context of her work "Institut du Monde Arabe (IAW) Window-Wallpaper". For the term of an exhibition, she covered the window spaces of the Galerie Zwinger in Berlin with paper, on which facsimiles of the facade structure of the Institute of the Arab World were printed in digital pigmentation. Her model was an isolated window element, which, designed by Jean Nouvel himself, is on longterm display in the Centre Georges Pompidou in Paris. Only when they are applied do the graphic elements combine into an identifiable pattern. And in addition, the paper display shifts the threshhold between interior and exterior space: from the outside one could look into the gallery space through circular cutouts as if through spyholes. Seen from the inside, the facsimile functions as a transparent wallpaper or a curtain.

20–23 A showroom is a temporary place, which is used by the fashion world as a meeting place during the Prêt-à-Porter shows in Paris, Milan, London or New York. In the Institute of the Arab World, which was from the start intended to be a "shop window for the Arab world", fashion shows often take place as well. Since the 11 September 2001, commercial leasing of the premises has actually been particularly sought after. Bettina Allamoda covered a kiosk from German Democratic Republic days with the pattern of the Institute of the Arab World for her work, "Institute of the Arab World/Showroom". Passers-by could peep straight through several openings into the interior. Alongside a series of various interiors of IAW-showrooms, posters of the current spring collection by John Galliano could be seen. In this way, Bettina Allamoda was commenting on the voyeuristic interest in the Arab world, but also on the tendency to have old and worn-out things disappear behind screens.

Alsop Design Ltd.

In 1979, the architect Will Alsop opened his own office in London. Today, Alsop Design Ltd. has several branches around the world, located in Rotterdam as well as in Toronto, Singapore and Shanghai.
www.alsoparchitects.com

24/25 As the studios and teaching rooms of the Ontario College of Art and Design have been arranged above the pre-existing building in a steelframe construction in order to connect the adjacent park with the street space, the two-storey extension of the Sharp Centre for Design appears to be floating 26 metres above the ground. Window openings cut in different formats create, in conjunction with square and rectangular slabs of aluminium, a pattern of black and white "pixels". This makes the new building appear like a closed box and at the same time the pattern disguises its dimensions and weight from the observer. The project was created in co-operation with the firm of architects Robbie/Young +Wright.

26/27 A protruding, partly transparent roof and walls made of wire mesh cloak the building of the Children's Centre, constructed from recycled shipping containers, as well as its outside play areas. Coloured "pastilles" in acrylic lend a playful air to the "Fawood Children's Centre" in one of London's outer suburbs. These "pastilles" were inserted into the thinner stainless steel mesh in the upper wall area. This resulted in a three-dimensional pattern and in a colour rhythm, which endows the interior with a varying range of lighting moods.
The "Colorium" office building at the harbour of Düsseldorf gains its pictorial presence through a complex patchwork of coloured glass elements. From just seventeen different types of panelling, arranged with a continued shifting of alignment, a sort of mosaic was created, which spans the entire length of the facade.

Birgit Antoni

Birgit Antoni is an artist and lives in Cologne.
www.birgitantoni.de

28–33 Birgit Antoni has been concerning herself for years with the structure of circles. As she draws the circles freehand – without the aid of a template – onto canvas, each resulting circle is different from the previous one. To make the minimal differences become visible, Birgit Antoni works with image pairs. It is only in the correspondence of pendants, which seem to be identical at first sight, that the differences in detail, as in the overall composition, can be noted. Whilst she cultivates deliberate "non-repetition", Antoni adheres to the "exemplary" law of symmetry and seriality.

Haleh Anvari

Haleh Anvari is an artist and works in various media like conceptual photography and video. She lives in Teheran.

34/35 A chador does not always have to be black. If it is traditionally patterned and made of materials in vivid colours, it takes on another meaning. The Iranian photo and video artist Haleh Anvari, who designs spotted, floral and striped chadors and records them in photographs, provides a reminder that the ornamentation that has been finding an application in Iran for decades, above all as a programme of images exploited for propaganda, because it symbolises a social order in which the individual is subservient to the community, can also take on distinctly subversive traits. A turquoise or orange-red chador is no longer the instrument, only tolerable with difficulty, of oppression by orthodox religious adherents, but doubtlessly also an object of fashion. And that can change at any time.

John M Armleder

John M Armleder is an artist and lives in Geneva. He is a Professor of Painting at the Academy of Fine Arts in Brunswick.

36/37 John M Armleder does not fabricate but locate. In the course of this, he reaches back to whatever is already available: to images and objects, which he thinks are so good that they deserve reproduction. This is why he has been a proponent of appropriation art since the 1980s. In art too, so his insight goes, there are no innovations any more but only second-hand experience. This he welcomes as an advantage, however, as an intensification of complexity. For, through repetition, art becomes décor, stage set, echo. And this is just what prevents you having to identify with it. In the Galleria d'Arte Moderna e Contemporanea in Bergamo he exhibited the work "Voltes IV" in 2005, a target composed of neon light. It makes art movements like Zero, op art und minimal art come alive again. And it can also be simply enjoyed as an attractive form in light and space.

38/39 "There is no doubt that I am primarily a painter," says John M Armleder. This is insofar astonishing, as he had already become a talking point by not only offering for sale hand signed originals but templates complete with instructions and certificate of authenticity as well. With "Arsenic" and "Anthophyllite", Armleder was still getting involved personally. The names he gave to the pictures are not listed in any dictionary of borrowed words; instead, everyone is familiar with the motifs: floral patterns. Even Andy Warhol, in his time, thought nothing of producing pictures of flowers – because people enjoy them. Warhol realized that art is not least a business. And John M Armleder sees, like Andy Warhol, no reason why he should not affirm that he is in the art business.

Atelier Tekuto

Atelier Tekuto is a firm of architects that was founded in Tokyo in 1995 by Yasuhiro Yamashita.
www.tekuto.com

40/41 "Cell Brick" is the name of a house that Atelier Tekuto developed in 2004. The appeal of "Cell Brick", a three-storey dwelling for a designer and her two children situated in a suburb of Tokyo comes from its unity of construction and pattern. Ceramic-coated steel elements form the exterior walls. Several of these "bricks" were welded together to create larger elements and then screwed together to form the individual walls. Viewed from the outside, the boxes used show a flat chessboard pattern; but in contrast to their exterior flatness, on the interior, they provide useful storage space in the small house with its rather spartan appearance.

B

Baumschlager & Eberle

Baumschlager & Eberle is a firm of architects that was founded in Lochau (Austria) in 1984 by Carlo Baumschlager and Dietmar Eberle.
www.Baumschlager-Eberle.com

42/43 The architects chose a contrastive parquet in different tones of Canadian maple for the foyer of the Münchner Rück insurance company. And they used it to cover the walls and ceilings as well. With this uniform treatment, they break with the conventional division of space and irritate the observer. In addition, the simple horizontal pattern reinforces the dynamically perspectival effect of the extremely extended space. An almost surreal effect.

Thomas Bayrle

Thomas Bayrle is an artist and lives in Frankfurt am Main. As a Professor for Fine Art at the Städelschule in Frankfurt am Main, Thomas Bayrle was from 1975 to 2004 a model and inspiration for his students for decades.

44–49 Stop and Go amid the flow of signs: one thing lines up with the other, duplicates and reproduces itself, goes on proliferating and forming networks, until the channel is full and the area too small, until the always identical symbols are so many that the store overflows. But it is not that simple excess rules here. What lines up, interweaves and accumulates, all that suddenly generates, out of the midst of its multiple selves, a "superform". From the increasing mass a camel forms out of camels, a Chevrolet out of Chevrolets, the face of Orson Welles comes together from lots of portraits. Here the small is always identical with the big, the particular submits to the general, the individual disappears in favour of an ornamentation en masse. In this way, patterns find their meaning and become parts of a great image.

Vanessa Beecroft

Vanessa Beecroft, born in Genua, is an artist and lives in New York.
www.vanessabeecroft.com

50–53 The photographs of Vanessa Beecroft document her performances, which are meticulously planned and thought through down to the last detail. Uniformed, made-up, coiffed and most often naked, female models are presented over a period of several hours to an audience interested in art. Weeks of casting, of negotiations with producers, organisers, photographers and film crews lead up to the implementation of such an image concept. In 2001, Vanessa Beecroft took up a pattern which she had found in the room in Pescara: a pattern of black and white stripes designed by Giò Ponti in 1936. The artist borrows the graphic play of white and black stripes and extends it to the body of two women, one white and one black. Through engaging with a system of decoration, the image of the female, the female as image, and our understanding of race and gender are being challenged.

Jurgen Bey

Jurgen Bey studied at the Design Academy in Eindhoven. In 1998, he founded an office for design in Rotterdam.
www.jurgenbey.nl

54/55 The designer frequently uses opulent floral patterns, which play with local references. Accordingly, Jurgen Bey chose the sort of floral motifs typical of Delft faïence for the foyer of a Dutch insurance company. The patterns derived from decorative and useful plants are not only reminiscent of design traditions typical of the country, but also of the beginnings of the company, which originated in a cooperative incorporation of farmers and gardeners. By contrast, with a bench in Tokyo, which is composed like an installation of various chairs, he refers to East Asian floral motifs – and likewise with the chairs for a café in St. Petersburg, which are covered with the same floral pattern.

Tord Boontje

Tord Boontje is a designer and lives in Bourg-Argental.
www.tordboontje.com

56–61 The floral pattern is Tord Boontje's subject matter. He is fascinated by the fact that the precise execution of those details belonging to past epochs' art and crafts can now be transferred, with the help of new technologies, into serial production. In addition, arts and crafts of the past and concepts from the world of fashion find their way into his approach to interior decoration. Hence, overflowing ornaments with numerous tendrils spawn coverings and "dresses" for furniture with textile qualities made of, for instance, wool felt, silk or the paper-like synthetic material, Tyvek. His metal lamp "Garland" and its Tyvek-offshoot "Midsummer Light" throw the blossoms wrapped around them as shadows onto the wall.

Bosshard Vaquer Architekten

Bosshard Vaquer Architekten is a firm of architects that was founded in Zurich in 2001 by Daniel Bosshard and Meritxell Vaquer i Fernández.
www.bosshardvaquer.com

62/63 When they were remodelling the viewing halls of a Zurich cemetery from 1917, the architects decided to restore the room to its original state. They combined several small rooms. For their wall design they reached back to the historical decorations and from small details developed patterns, which cover all the walls and ceilings. From frieze of palmettes, computerised modification generated a wall-filling pattern, which appears astonishing modern and scarcely allows the historical model to be discerned.

Linda Bradford

Linda Bradford is a graphic designer and lives in New York.
www.lindabradford.net

64–67 In all her works, Linda Bradford creates harmonies of colour and spatial illusions. „Thanks to the versatility afforded by digital algorithms, the harmonic potential of colour can be arranged in illusory space, inviting viewers to orient themselves to the aesthetic potential of space itself", she comments. The digital studies are meant to lead shortly to a series of illuminated objects, in which this illusion is further emphasised by the increased dynamics of the light.

Stefan Bressel

Stefan Bressel is an artist and lives in Frankfurt am Main.

68–71 Stefan Bressel's works each consist of two pictures completing each other, where each relates to its pendant as a mirror image. Borrowing from Andy Warhol, Steffen Bressel has been concentrating for the last few years on a camouflage pattern. The camouflage pattern, which was introduced in 1975 by the American military under the name "Woodland" and is still in use today, is based on a colour catalogue, which imitates the appearance of vegetation in all seasons and is supposed to make the contours of the human figure and the objects, that are covered with this pattern, disappear. In a paradoxical twist, Stefan Bressel sees it that a pattern, which serves the military as camouflage, stands out above all optically. He has recently been using this principle of painting for murals. So he found an ideal place for his game with patterns and series in the octagonal pavilion of Schloss Molberg.

Persijn Broersen & Margit Lukács

Persijn Broersen and Margit Lukács are designers and live in Amsterdam.
www.pmpmpm.com

72–75 In their work "Black Light", the designers Persijn Broersen and Margit Lukács engage with an essential aspect of patterns: they point out the paradoxical situation that elements appearing successively in an indiscriminate series can simultaneously represent order and chaos. The idea behind their design is originated in mountainous terrain in Spain, where they noted the ambiguous nature of the indigenous plants: on the one hand, these plants appear symmetrical and ordered within themselves, but as a whole they often form a chaotically proliferating space. The pattern "BlackLight" reflects this experience – particularly in its walkable version, with which the designers lined the rooms of a gallery space in Haarlem.

Stefanie Bürkle

Stefanie Bürkle is an artist and city explorer.
The project "Beirut Berlin", a comparison of two cities divided after a war, and "Eiscafé Venezia" are some of her most recent works.
Stefanie Bürkle lives in Berlin.

76–81 Demolition is threatening for the Palast der Republik in Berlin, an architectural showpiece from GDR days and a symbol of East German identity. But Stefanie Bürkle has found a way to enable the patterns of its copper glass facade to survive. She is producing rolls of palace-wallpaper. And she is wallpapering a complete wall in each of selected Berlin workrooms with it. Figures from public life like Hortensia Völckers, Klaus Biesenbach and Matthias Flügge have taken part in this action, furnished their offices with the "Berlin Wallpaper" and have had their portrait done by Stefanie Bürkle. Taken from a public space into a private one and transformed from an architectural covering into an image, the facade loses its representative function and becomes décor.

C

Claudia Caviezel

Claudia Caviezel is a textile designer and lives in St. Gallen.
www.ccdc.ch

82/83 Claudia Caviezel's degree thesis for the Lucerne School of Art+Design is a work of design that is entitled "tape it". In several design sketches, she introduces approaches as much to fashion collections as to interior furnishings, in which conventional techniques for cutting, sewing and production are replaced by temporary connections like adhesive tape in the case of this work. "I manufacture products, which are not supposed to fail straightaway over the propensity for perfection", the textile designer Claudia Caviezel says.

Chalet 5

The designers Karin Wälchli und Guido Reichlin have been co-operating in Zurich under the name of Chalet 5 since 1995.
www.chalet5.ch

84–89 When carpet makers in the Orient change their work place, they often introduce patterns from their home into an already existing context and change it as a result – in German this is called "Musterverschleppung" – pattern-grabbing. Karin Wälchli and Guido Reichlin of Chalet 5 refer to this phenomenon and add their own ideas, when they use this term for groupings of their works. "sPaGaT" (The Splits) is part of the grouping "Musterverschleppung II": What at first sight seems unsystematic reveals the regularity of its lines when observed more closely. The works "EastWest" and "Speedfresh" are part of "Musterverschleppung III", in which spatial shapes come close to three-dimensionality.

Claesson Koivisto Rune

The Swedish designpartnership Claesson Koivisto Rune is a firm of architects and designers founded in Stockholm in 1995 by Mårten Claesson, Eero Koivisto and Ola Rune.
www.claesson-koivisto-rune.se

90/91 The "Sfera Building" culture house in Kyoto, with its gallery, bookshop, café and restaurant is meant to be a reminder of local traditions, yet be, at the same time, contemporary in its design. Titanium panels were fitted in front of the facade and conceal the building like a Japanese screen wall. The irregular, transparent pattern of incountable holes repeats itself. Only when the pattern is seen from a distance does it display a graphical pattern made up of innumerable leaves.

D

Wim Delvoye

Wim Delvoye is an artist and lives in Ghent.
He works in various media like sculpture, photography and installation.
www.cloaca.be

92–95 The Belgian Wim Delvoye evokes idiosyncrasies, that is: circumstances, in which the observer vacillates for a moment between fascination and disgust. Décors are for him a sign of beauty and of terror. He, therefore, has tiles manufactured, on which the traditional pattern of Delft stoneware can be recognised, albeit composed of photographed excrement. He detracts from his hommage to the wonderful marble floor of the Renaissance with the help of ham, sausage, salami and mortadella. And that ornamentation is not only suspected of a crime, but can also be employed as an ironic commentary on a general faith in technology, Wim Delvoye demonstrates by means of excavators, mixers or cranes, which are decorated all over with engraved webs of tendrils.

E

Erick van Egeraat associated architects

This firm of architects has been known as Erick van Egeraat associated architects since 1995.
It has offices in Rotterdam as well as in London, Moscow, Budapest und Prague.
www.eea-architects.com

96/97 The town hall of Alphen aan den Rijn in the Netherlands responds with its curving facade and its varying levels to the heterogeneous structures of its surroundings. The Meeting Room of the town hall rears up conspicuously over the entrance area. A pattern of leaves covers the entire glass facade. Photos of the trees on the building site were developed on the computer for that. The screen prints are applied as sunscreens to the inside of the glass panes in differing thicknesses according to the particular compass bearings.

F

Parastou Forouhar

Parastou Forouhar was born in Teheran and came to Germany in 1991.
She is an artist and lives in Offenbach am Main.
www.parastou-forouhar.de

98–101 "Eslimi" is a Persian word for ornamentation. It denotes a certain sort of tendril-figure in carpet production. Parastou Forouhar has been concerned for years with the various functions, which patterns and ornamentation take on in Iran: patterns are signs of the beautiful and the terrible. She has photographically enlarged the floral pattern, which is woven into the deep black chador, to make it visible. And the unscrupulous torturers, who are still active in the country, in which she grew up, she consigned to a carpet, the pattern of which can, at first sight, be outright pleasurable. "Eslimi" is what she calls a graphic construction, which is able to conceal its origins in objective reality so skillfully that without the title you would not latch onto it: "Genital Series" and "Fork Series" can be read there as a small addition. A few words are enough, and already the apparently abstract pattern becomes a battleground, where it is a case of life and death and the relationship between the sexes.

Future Systems

The firm of architects was founded in London in 1979 by Jan Kaplicky and Amanda Levete.
www.future-systems.com

102/103 In an extremely heterogeneous context, "Selfridges" department store stands out with its rounded, sculptural form amid the main traffic routes and the buildings of the postwar era. With a dynamically curving facade it reacts to the various buildings neighbouring "Selfridges" department store. 15,000 aluminium plates cover the whole, blue painted concrete facade like a second skin. They form a reflective pattern that emphasises the elegant curves and lends the entire building an astonishing lightness.

G

Daan van Golden
Daan van Golden is an artist and lives in Schiedam.

104/105 Daan van Golden finds his pictorial images in his immediate surroundings: in the kitchen or in the clothes cupboard. Since the time he spent in Japan in the 1960s, the artist paints, with precision and true to detail, what everyone knows:hankies, table cloths and towels. In this way, he is released from the necessity of inventing anything. Instead, he can concentrate on accomplishing his daily handiwork, brushstroke by brushstroke. His still lifes celebrate the unassuming and the everyday. And they show how endlessly prolific repetition can be.

H

Klaus Haapaniemi
Klaus Haapaniemi is an illustrator and lives in London.
www.klaush.com

106–111 For the Italian fashion label Bantam, Klaus Haapaniemi developed a fabric with silk embroidery, which appears to have been hand made, as well as a top produced by means of a laser cut technique, which looks as if it consisted of nothing but a pattern peeled off its background. Alongside fashion items Haapaniemi designs illustrations for magazines and books, in which he links the psychedelic style of the 1960's with inspirations from children's literature.

Elke Haarer
Elke Haarer is an artist and lives in Nuremberg.

112–117 Painting is not any more what it once was. That is why Elke Haarer investigates which functions painting and its legitimate offspring are meanwhile taking over as a matter of course. So Elke Haarer is one of her own accord left the classical tableau picture behind and demonstrates her artistic competence in the sphere of applied art: she designs patterns for wallpapers, she takes on the colour coordination of offices, restaurants and waiting rooms, and she is active as a shop window and facade designer. As an artist, she is, however, certainly well aware that décors are not only form, but also have meaning. And with that games can be played. Hence a wallpaper can be more than a wall covering. The offset prints with which Elke Haarer furnishes a room show the motif of water lilies and bear the name "Giverny". Claude Monet, who lived in Giverny and interpreted the world as a pure phenomenon of light, sends his regards. Yet right there, where we suppose the beginning of modernist painting, there lurks also the logo of the consumer world. It is not only the name of Monet that is connected to the image of the water lily, but also the image of the sports goods manufacturer Adidas.

Tobias Hauser
The artist Tobias Hauser lives in Berlin.

118/119 Tobias Hauser's works are situated in the undefined space somewhere between sculpture, relief and painting. The three wall-objects in the classical picture format each consists of four painted wooden lattices. Overlapping, they multiply the pictorial field, induce the gaze to plumb the depths, but block the vision. There is no doubt that this is a result of well-crafted precision work. Yet beyond these components of production aesthetics, these works also open a discursive field: from the titles "Der Morgen", "Der Tag" and "Der Abend" can be discerned how they refer to Philipp Otto Runge's paintings of the same name, a complex allegorising of the stage of life, the growth and ageing process of nature and humanity. In this way the finely carved bifurcations, bringing entwined tendrils to mind, are a timely interpretation of developing and decaying.

Geka Heinke
Geka Heinke is an artist and lives in Berlin.

120–125 Geka Heinke finds her motifs in everyday surroundings: they are objects like double windows, coconut matting, bathroom mirrors, lamps and wallpapers. Much of it points to the typical aesthetics of furnishing from the 1960s and 1970s, but also to the typical equipping of rooms in the former GDR. Yet where décor dwells is a place people have long since quit. So it is not a face appearing in the mirror, but the tile pattern on the opposite wall. And should something like life ensue in the living room, we cannot make it out, because a patterned curtain blocks our sight. So patterns function

with Geka Heinke less as harmless decorative elements than as a metaphorical scheme of the uncanny and the hermetic.

Herzog & de Meuron
Herzog & de Meuron is a firm of architects founded in Basel in 1978 by Jacques Herzog und Pierre de Meuron.
www.gsd.harvard.edu/people/faculty/herzog/projects.html

126/127 For the library of the Technical University of Eberswalde, a sort of screen-printing process was used to transfer the images directly onto the concrete of the facade. By means of a chemical treatment, the concrete stayed soft in parts and could subsequently be sluiced out. In this way, a relief took shape on the outside wall. It was completed with photo motifs, all chosen by the artist Thomas Ruff and printed onto glass. Horizontally, the images repeat apparently endlessly and coalesce into a pattern, which covers the facade.

Hild und K
The firm of architects was founded in 1992 by Andreas Hild and Tillmann Kaltwasser.
Since Kaltwasser's death in 1999, the firm has been trading under the name of Hild und K Architekten with Dionys Ottl as a partner.
www.hildundk.de

128/129 For a rural residence in Aggstal (Germany), the architects chose a light-coloured whitewashed facade with a diamond pattern in brick. The geometrical pattern does not end, however, exactly at the corner, but is continued on around the edges of the building. This is how the architects play on the image of a traditional wall.

130/131 For the wall design of a meeting room Hild and K chose a classical technique. A drawing was scored into the plaster surface and later filled with coloured plaster, rubbed down and waxed. How far the subtle pattern can be made out depends, in this case, very much on the light conditions.
The Bavarian Research and Technology Centre for Sports Science needed a highly flexible building capable of being freely partitioned across its ground plan. Accordingly the load bearing outer walls of the central structure got a facade with regular perforations and only two window openings. The strict network is enveloped with a striped pattern made of various overlaid coats of varnish.

Steven Holl Architects
Steven Holl Architects was founded in 1974 by Steven Holl in New York.
www.stevenholl.com

132–135 Steven Holl uses a pattern composed of small elements to break up the traditional grid facade of the Massachusetts Institute of Technology's Simmons Hall. On photographs, the building seems gigantic, until one understands that three rows of windows belong to one storey and that the building has only ten floors. Window embrasures in different colours liven up the severe, regular pattern of the pierced facades. At the same time, openings, bays and amorphous areas in the window frontage made of solid concrete serve as irritation. The irregular areas correspond to freely formed communal spaces, each of which spans several floors. Steven Holl takes advantage of the clearcut pattern of the construction to disturb it in numerous ways, creating a complex facade as a result.

I

Toyo Ito & Associates, Architects
In 1971, Toyo Ito founded his own studio Urban Robot in Tokyo, which has been trading under the name of Toyo Ito & Associates, Architects since 1979.
www.toyo-ito.co.jp

136–139 The facade of the Performing Arts Center in Matsumoto is characterised by a playful treatment of the contrasts of bright and dark and lightness and weightiness. The bright patches seem like reflections on the walls of the foyer. The irregularly shaped glass elements themselves, however, are the sources of light. On the exterior

facade, too, these "inclusions" create a playful pattern in the concrete facade, which emphasises its sweeping shape.

J

Dale Jones-Evans Architecture
Dale Jones-Evans founded his firm of architects in 1984 in Surry Hills, New South Wales, Australia.
www.dje.com.au

140/141 As protection against the burning Australian sun, the architects developed an outer sunscreen made of rusty steel elements. Perhaps surprisingly, they point out Chinese influences in the pattern. Europeans are rathermore reminded of motifs from the Orient and of a very robust version of Jean Nouvel's facade for the Institute of the Arab World.

Hella Jongerius
Hella Jongerius is a designer and lives in Rotterdam.
www.jongeriuslab.com

142/143 For her series of bowls, Hella Jongerius has looked into the historical décors of Nymphenburg, the porcelain manufacturers, and brought to light a few of the animal-figure designs from the firm's archive. She comments on the naturalistic sculptures with traces of the production process. Hence, there are dabs of colour and hand-written insignia around the edges, and the patterned areas extend like fragments from other epochs across parts of the objects.

144/145 For the "Sampler Blankets", the designer found inspiration from the fabric pattern collection of the Cooper-Hewitt Design Museum in New York. Her blankets show, on the one hand, characteristics of traditional patterns and methods, but on the other hand, they are also marked by modern needle-punch technology, with which hundreds of needles apply the threads simultaneously to front and reverse sides of the fabric.

146/147 With the name "Repeat", Hella Jongerius programmatically designates, on the other hand, a fabric design, in which the sequences of repetition for the individual elements are extremely long. And so it is, even at large scale, almost impossible to choose two identical sections.

Jourda Architectes
Jourda Architectes is a firm of architects founded in 1998 by Françoise Hélène Jourda, with offices in Lyon and Paris.
www.jourda-architectes.com

148–151 A manufacturing hall with a separate wing for offices was constructed on the margins of an industrial zone for a manufacturer of office chairs. Viewed from the outside, these buildings with their elegant glass facades disappear between two monumental walls alongside. The architects describe them as "rock walls". From prefabricated concrete parts just under 10 metres in height and 2 metres in width they developed by means of a simple variation of alignment a three dimensional pattern, which gains additional structure through its bolt fastenings.

K

Klein Dytham Architecture
Klein Dytham Architecture is a firm of architects and designers founded in Tokyo in 1991 by Astrid Klein und Mark Dytham.
www.klein-dytham.com

152/153 The wedding chapel in Kobuchizawa (Japan), which is part of a hotel complex, is composed of two half-bowls or "leaves", as the architects call them. Perforated and fitted out with 4,700 acrylic lenses, the pattern of holes in the white steel bowl is reminiscent of broderie anglaise, particularly when closed at night. During the day, when it is open, the lenses project their pattern like a shadow onto a white membrane. The architects use the backs of the benches to create a similarly diffuse image. Here, floral motifs in a light green were inserted into acrylic glass and melt with the view of the water.

Silvia Knüppel & Damien Regamey

Silvia Knüppel and Damien Regamey are product designers.
Damien Regamey lives in Switzerland and Silvia Knüppel in Karlsruhe.
www.page75.ch

154/155 In sport, everything is subordinated to the dictate of efficiency: not only the athletes, also the sport equipment has to achieve high performance. Silvia Knüppel und Damien Regamey undermine the aesthetics of forms tested in wind tunnels and hyperintelligent materials when they lend volleyball and table-tennis nets the appearance of patterned crochet tablecloths. With their project "Homesick", which was honoured by the Women Volvo Sports Design Award in 2005, they bring back all of what the perfect world of sport has expelled: ornamentation, handiwork and whatever is bound by tradition.

Takehito Koganezawa

Takehito Koganezawa was born in Tokyo.
He is an artist and has lived in Berlin since 1994.

156–159 The Japanese concept of "ma" denotes the void, nothingness. Takehito Koganezawa's thinking revolves around the "ma". "I really want to see nothingness in an exact way, but what I can find always has meaning. So I try to wash out the meaning from an object," he once said. Hence the series of crayon drawings, devoted to the appearance of insects, carries the significant title "Superficial Blackhole". Takehito Koganezawa avoids firm contour lines. What interests him just as much as the shape of the beetle, which organises itself from lots of coloured dots, is the empty space between these dots. The white paper is ground and interstice – and not least a representation of nothingness.

Peter Kogler

Peter Kogler is an artist and lives in Vienna.
He is a Professor of Art und Digital Media at the Vienna Academy of Fine Arts.
www.kogler.net

160/161 Peter Kogler is using the possibilities of the computer to generate novel ornamentation and patterns. Hence, for the documenta 9 he designed, for example, wallpapers, which created the impression that ants were marching in hordes, but well-ordered ones, on the walls, the ceiling and the floor of the exhibition hall. Or he hung as wallpaper some pictures of gigantic pipes, which symbolised the invisible interior, the veins, arteries and innards of a human being, the water pipes lying under the plaster and the virtual data highways, on which the bytes zoom along with the speed of light. In the Kunsthaus Bregenz, Peter Kogler changed the walls of the museum into huge projection surfaces, on which what was forced out of fine art in the 19th century, returns with enormous energy: ornamentation. On the screens there could be observed the development history of ornamentation: the shift from the braided band to the streak pattern. Not least through their size, such pictures exercise an immense fascination on the observer: here patterns are conceived as expansion, as something bourgeoning.

Yayoi Kusama

Yayoi Kusama is an artist and works in various media, like sculpture, painting, installation, and as a novelist.
She lives in Tokyo and New York.
www.yayoi-kusama.jp

162–165 Yayoi Kusama, born in Japan in 1929, moved to New York at the end of the 1950s. There she attracted attention in the 1960s with space-consuming installations: the artist did not only cover screens but also ceilings, floors and walls with net-like structures and dots. In actions, in which she painted for forty to fifty hours without a break, she transformed the concrete, physical space with the aid of décor into a psychedelic space seemingly stretching into limitlessness. In the 1970s, Yayoi Kusama returned to Japan. Only at the end of the 1990s was her consistent treatment of décor and space rediscovered and celebrated in the shape of exhibitions and publications. In connection with a retrospective, which took place in the Kunstverein Braunschweig, Yayoi Kusama once again employed the principle of the multiplication, repetition and disinhibiting of space by décor and mirror effects and created "Dots Obsession".

L

Lab Architecture Studio

Lab Architecture Studio was founded in London in 1994 by Peter Davidson und Donald L. Bates.
After being awarded first prize in the Federation Square competition, they opened a second office in Melbourne.
www.labarchitecture.com

166–169 Federation Square, a square of 3.6 hectares with a variety of new buildings used for cultural and commercial activities, emerged quicklyas a new and lively centre of public life in Melbourne. The National Gallery of Victoria, the Australian Centre for the Moving Image and a radio- and television station are the main attractions. But the open spaces, too, which have been configured for concerts and other events, attract up to 35,000 visitors per day. The fractal geometry of the facades allows for a surprising variety in design and consequently for a differentiation of the individual buildings. Basic triangular elements, made of sandstone, zinc sheeting and glass, form fan-shaped modules, which are combined in turn to form larger panels. Although the individual parts have been industrially prefabricated, the patterns achieve an unusual complexity. Changes in material, in proportions and in the three-dimensional alignment create a confusing diversity of facades – something which would have been unthinkable just a few years ago.

Rüdiger Lainer

Rüdiger Lainer founded his own office in Vienna in 1985.
www.lainer.at

170/171 The terracing of the multi-family dwelling on the margin of Grinzing refers to the surrounding landscape, to the hills and embankments of the Vienna Woods. A structure made of cast aluminium, which encases the entire building with a pattern reminiscent of plants, was erected in front of the facade. This second layer ties together the various apartments to a whole and thus reconciles them to the neighbouring single-family dwellings.

172/173 The office and fitness centre in the Hüttendorfstrasse in Vienna is located in an industrial building, which was erected at the beginning of the last century according to the plans of the architect and designer Walter Sabatka (1888–1970). In 2003, the Ruediger Lainer architectural practise added an extension and a roof superstructure to this antecedent building. An extension and a roof superstructure have been added to a historic industrial building. For structural reasons, a light construction of steel and prefabricated concrete walls as well as a covering of cast aluminium slabs were chosen. Imprints of branches and leaves, initially moulded in clay, lend a strong relief to the basic modules. Serial repetition then results in a complex pattern of natural, dynamic surface texture and a severe, artificial order.

Abigail Lane

The designer Abigail Lane is in charge of the designgroup Showroom Dummies and lives in London.
www.showroomdummies.com

174–177 For her interior furnishing, Abigail Lane draws decorative aspects from natural catastrophes and symbols of death. Volcanic eruptions and storms in large scale reveal the dark side of the motif-based wallpapers so beloved in the 1970s and overshadow living and bedrooms with a Gothic aesthetic. The photographic wall coverings only become patterns through mirror-imaging – different from the small-format, graphic elements derived from simple silhouettes, with which Abigail Lane likewise works.

Léon Wohlhage Wernik Architekten

The office Léon Wohlhage Wernik Architekten was founded by Hilde Léon and Konrad Wohlhage in Berlin in 1987.
www.leonwohlhagewernik.de

178/179 The architects chose a red sandstone for the facade of the new building of the Indian Embassy. This material was also used in the generous public spaces of the building's interior. There, stone lattices in metal frames serve as mobile partitions. In India, these are traditionally used as windows or screens. Here, the customary patterns known as "jalis" (English: nets) were enlarged to maximum size.

Renée Levi

Renée Levi is an artist and lives in Basel.

180/181 Renée Levi has become known through large-scale spatial works: in a self-replicating gesture, she sprays fluorescent colours directly onto walls. In designing the facade of a communal district heating power station in Zürich-Oerlikon, she rejected a handwritten style in favour of the ornamental effect of repeating the figure 2. In a scaled relation to the human body, the dark green pattern structures the white walls, organises the intercalated volumes and lends the building the quality of a trademark.

Michael Lin

The artist Michael Lin lives and works in Taipei and Paris.

182–187 Michael Lin is still today preoccupied with the patterns of his childhood. The artist today uses traditional floral décors, which he knows from cushion covers and counterpanes from provincial Taiwan, in new contexts. Stylised blossoms and buds – enlarged oversize – surface again in international museums as space-consuming installations. Whether as landscapes for lounging with giant cushions or as half-pipe for skateboarders, the enlarged patterns cover floors, walls and utilitarian objects. At the same time, he made his motifs unfamiliar by having them frequently reproduced so large that they are almost impossible to make out from close up. In the gigantic inner hall of the Stadhuis in Den Haag, observers can only make out the pattern chosen for the floor from the upper storeys. A further distancing arises from the surprising context in which the patterns were applied, for example, as advertising hoardings for an exhibition, as floor covering, which curves up the walls, or meanwhile as décor for furniture manufacturers.

M

Daniele Marques

In 1977, Daniele Marques founded his own office in Lucerne, which has been trading under the name of Marques AG since 1998.
www.marques.ch

188/189 The new building, with local government offices, workshops and the depot of the fire brigade in the Swiss municipality of Münsterlingen, combines extremely heterogeneous public functions. Nevertheless, the impression it gives on the outside is calm and uniform. Its slanted, charcoal coloured roof and the concrete facades toned in black enhance its compact appearance. Selecting crude boards of different widths for the planking created a sort of relief facade, which reminds of, among other things, the sunburnt wooden facades of the township.

Agnes Martin

Agnes Martin (1912–2004) hails from a Scottish pioneers family, which emigrated from the Isle of Skye to the Canadian West.
She was born in Maklin, Saskatchewan as a farmer's daughter and spent her youth in Vancouver;
in 1932, she migrated to the United States, where she taught at various colleges from 1947 to 1953.
In 1957, she moved to New York.
In 1967, she settled in New Mexico.

190/191 Agnes Martin comes at the end of the 1950s to the characteristic organisational form of her pictures, to the striped layering of straight, parallel, mostly horizontally extended lines and to the meshed overlaying of vertical and horizontal lines. In the mid 1960s, she takes over from the minimalists the non-hierarchical, centreless structuring of the pictorial surface, which has left any trace of illusionism behind. She often has recourse to a latticework structure, which releases her from the need to make a compositional decision. Agnes Martin comments that although her formats are square, the lattices are never absolutely so. They are rectangular, a little bit outside of a square. They shrink somewhat, she says, and points to a dissonance she did not plan from the outset. In her opinion, if she covers the surface of the square with rectangular forms, that highlights the weight of the square and destroys its power.

Thomas Mass

Thomas Mass is an artist and lives in Düsseldorf.

192/193 For the Malkasten in Düsseldorf, the premises of an artists' association, Thomas Mass developed a concept, which corresponded to the basic architectural structure of this building from the 1950s. He modified a photographic view of Frank Lloyd Wright's famous spiral in the Guggenheim Museum New York into a pattern, which he applied to a stairwell in Düsseldorf. In this way, he offers access to the relationship of painting and photography, of institution and individual artist, of illusory and concrete space.

194–197 When Thomas Mass paints or draws, then he descends into a web of lines. It is not the relationship of design and execution, not working on the model that interests him, but the accuracy, which can be gained from operating in the here and now. None of his decisions can be revised, no brushstroke undone. Line for line, dot for dot, Thomas Mass trusts his eye, the precision of his movements, the rhythm of his body. Hence there is no mathematical system underlying the patterns of his pictures, but the intuitive knowledge of how proportion, colour and form ideally relate to each other.

Bruce Mau

Bruce Mau is a graphic designer.
In 1985, he founded the office Bruce Mau Design Inc.
He lives in Toronto.
www.brucemaudesign.com

198–201 Three large sculptural rooflight-units crown the building complex, in which the Art Center College of Design in Pasadena has its premises. Their panes are made of resilient synthetic foil, for which Bruce Mau designed a decal in the form of a punch-card-like pattern. Areas of dot matrices overlay each other, break the light falling through them and, above all, signal under nocturnal illumination that visual design is what is going on under these roofs. Most of all, they transmit the illusion of depth – and that from a surface. MegaNano by Bruce Mau challenges the predictably static appearance of panel fabric with the introduction of two series of patterns each centered on a singular theme.

Paul Moss

Paul Moss lives in Newcastle, England.
He is an artist and co-founder of the Workplace Art Gallery Ltd. in Newcastle.

202/203 With his "Danger Paintings", Paul Moss gauges the gap, which yawns between fine and applied art. Because the striped ribbon his paintings are made of serves a practical purpose outside of the art context, Paul Moss uses the marker tape, which is employed on building sites and as a barrier. In White Cube Moss investigates the aesthetic effect of the pattern, which in the urban space warns of dangers.

Markus Moström

The Swedish designer Markus Moström runs a design firm in Stockholm.
He lives in Stockholm.
www.mostromdesign.se

204–207 The Swedish designer had already created for "Sfera Building" its graphic look. In 2005, he received a commission to design kimonos for the Japanese company. Under the title "Wrapping", he designed fabrics with notably flattened patterns, which only develop a three-dimensional effect on the body. Simple motifs from organic-seeming elements or stripes come across as if dispersed into individual pixels on the computer. The jagged contours of the rounded forms or the irregular patterns from elongated rectangles can also be read as references to traditional production methods. Then they conform to large-scale photos of patterns, which only allow their woven structure to be recognised in extreme enlargement.

N

Nägeli Architekten

Nägeli Architekten is a firm of architects that was founded in Berlin in 1998 by Walter Nägeli and Gudrun Sack.
www.naegeliarchitekten.de

208/209 For the single-family houses in Berlin nicknamed parquet buildings, wood was not only employed for construction with panel building modules, but also for the exterior cladding. Its fishbone pattern made of larch timber, borrowed from the interior, stresses the verticality of the tower-like living blocks standing amid lofty fir trees. At the same time, the unusual diagonal pattern creates a varied play of colour and light as well as a surprising spatial effect.

Carsten Nicolai

Carsten Nicolai is an artist, musician and producer.
He lives in Berlin.

210–213 Carsten Nicolai works at the juncture of art and natural science. In recent years, he has developed various methods to make phenomena like sound and light frequencies or electromagnetic fields visually apprehensible. In the framework of trial arrangements, Carsten Nicolai has, for instance, animated liquids with various frequencies of sound signals. In this way, the photo series "milch" came about. It shows in close-up the surface of milk, which is made to vibrate by rising frequencies. Whilst low tones produce unstructured images, high tones form rhythmically organised patterns.

Olaf Nicolai

Olaf Nicolai is an artist and lives in Berlin.

Olaf Nicolai reflects on perception processes. "Questions about forms, moods, attitudes and style are not a luxurious game with surfaces. They are questions about the organisational forms of activities", he says. In his works, which he realises in various media, it is not least a question of adopting what is commonplace, of shifting contexts and of the concomitant changing of meaning.

214/215 The poster quotes the motif of a drop of blood from the 16th century painting "Flagellation of Christ" by Jan Baegert. The blood-drop design in various sizes covers the poster, and the posters are displayed staggered in multiple layers throughout the space available. The stereotype treatment of the drop of blood moves the motif into the vicinity of decorative art.

216/217 Places surrounded by motorways and main roads are islands, cut off from the space around them. Olaf Nicolai sought out such a non-place, called an "eye" in the professional jargon of the traffic planners, when he was invited in 2004 to take part in the Heidenheim sculpture symposium. To make the blocked-in spot double, he covered the "eye" with a camouflage pattern, as developed by the military to ensure things are overlooked. With the help of a landscaping firm, Olaf Nicolai planted up the traffic island in a camouflage pattern consisting of 55,000 plants. Nature, therefore, no longer appeared as nature but as an artificial pattern, which imitates and mimics nature.

218/219 In 2000, starting out with the facade of a department store in Dresden, the facade design of which shows that in the 1960s there were attempts in the GDR to acquire the architectural language of forms from international modernity, Olaf Nicolai designed a lamp. It consists of 16 polyhedron elements and bears the name "Dresden 1968". In 2002, this construction then became the basis for a cover design: Olaf Nicolai returned to it when he designed the folder for "Rewind-Forward", a documentation of his projects.

Ateliers Jean Nouvel

In 1977, Jean Nouvel founded his first office of architects together with François Seigneur.
Today, the office in Paris is called Ateliers Jean Nouvel.
www.jeannouvel.fr

220/221 For the south facade of the Institute of the Arab World, a cultural centre with a museum and a library, Jean Nouvel chose a technically extravagant sunscreen. Mechanically adjustable elements open depending on the incidence of light like the aperture of a camera. On the one hand, these construction details filter the light as

in Arabian buildings, on the other hand, these screens achieve a pattern evocative of the Orient. In this, high-tech architecture and traditional patterns are united in an almost playful manner.

Fabio Novembre

Fabio Novembre is a designer and lives in Milan.
As Creative Director for Bisazza, he has designed widely noted showrooms for the company.
www.novembre.it

222–225 Whoever enters the lobby of the hotel "UNA Vittoria" in Florence is in for a surprise. Several spirals run through the foyer and so irritate the way the space is perceived. A huge loop, covered with a flower pattern, winds through the entrance area and ends at the reception counter. The curving form and the floral pattern, which is reminiscent of old brocade material, contrast with the severe crisscrossing in the small-segment mosaic. Where earlier the single stitches of embroidery or the threads of weaving formed an unassuming basic unit for the patterns, so it is today the pixels of the computer, which can break up a picture into square units and supply the construction drawings for the mosaics. The same astonishing contradictions mark the showroom for Bisazza in New York. Here the soft forms and abstracted floral patterns also consist of individual mosaic pieces. The loops serve this time as benches, and the floral pattern seems borrowed from art deco and is distantly reminiscent of Andy Warhol's flower pictures.

O

Office for Metropolitan Architecture

The Firm of architects was founded in 1977 in Rotterdam.
O.M.A.'s partners today are Rem Koolhaas, Josua Ramus, Ellen van Loon and Ole Scheeren.
O.M.A. has offices in Rotterdam, New York, Bejing.
www.oma.nl

226/227 The extremely contoured construction, with its characteristic projections and depressions, corresponds to the partitioning of the building into various zones. The public library is organised around different service areas, a "living room" and conventional workstations. The diamond-pattern of the suspended facade enhances the dynamic effect of the dramatic slant of the wall. And the graphic diagonal lines have been precisely extended over the entire facade.

228/229 The McCormick-Tribune Campus Center for the Illinois Institute of Technology does not in the least conform to the expectations of wild collages of materials either, for which the Office for Metropolitan Architecture was once known. Here, the influence of Mies van der Rohe, who planned this campus in the fifties, is obvious. The organisation of the glass facades is a subtle reminder of its famous models. A portrait of Mies van der Rohe covers the entire entrance area in a much bolder fashion. And a closer look reveals a pattern of pictograms, which form the grid of the photo out of bright and dark dots.

P

Susanne Paesler

Susanne Paesler is an artist and lives in Berlin.

230–235 Susanne Paesler has never taken leave of traditional painting, the rigorous, lonely business with brush and colour. And yet her pictures allow insight into the way digital image manipulation has changed painting. The pictures we see every day have already gone through various stages of transformation: they are reproduced, dissolve into dot-matrices, are retouched via Photoshop. "The electronic image manipulation programmes return photography to the status of painting", says Susanne Paesler. "Photography has not got a reliable reference to reality any more, but can generate images like painting." That painting is, all the same, the dominant discipline, because it owns its own constructedness, Susanne Paesler demonstrates as she offers all the illusion effects of trompe l'œil. With the help of templates, she repeats what already exists: geometrical material patterns, floral patterns from the fashion world, pixilated patterns from the digital world, but also the gestural patterns of a Jackson Pollock. By applying coachpaint to aluminium, Susanne Paesler creates pictures with a textureless surface – as we know them from photography. And even the artist's signature, which, in the old-established manner, Susanne Paesler sets in the right-hand, lower corner of the picture, is no longer the handwritten confirmation of her own activity, but the result of repetition based on a template.

Blinky Palermo

Blinky Palermo, whose conventional name was Peter Heisterkamp, was born in Leipzig in 1943.
From 1962 to 1967, he studied at the Düsseldorf Academy of Art, with Bruno Goller and Joseph Beuys among other people.
In 1972, he took part in the documenta 5.
Blinky Palermo died on Kurumba in the Maldives in 1977, aged 33.

236/237 Like Imi Knoebel and Rainer Ruthenbeck, Blinky Palermo looked in the 1960s to the potential of constructivist art. At the same time he looked for means and ways of harmonising elements from the realms of High and Low Culture. So he used, for instance, industrially produced materials to simulate the effects of Color-Field-Painting. On the 1965 canvas "Straight", 38 narrow strips running vertically in the colours red, blue and yellow overlie 32 equally narrow horizontal bands. In this way, a rectangular mesh comes about, which covers the rectangular surface of the painting in a non-hierarchical Allover. The result is a flickering pulsation. And with "Flipper" too, the composition of the picture corresponds to a freely extendable network. Blinky Palermo found the inspiration to use a red-blue-white diamond pattern in the objective world: the side-panel of a pinball machine in the artist's local pub served as a model.

Architects Patterson

Architects Patterson is a firm of architects that was founded in 1988 by Andrew Patterson in Auckland, New Zealand, later partnership with Peter Eising.
www. architectspatterson.co.nz

238/239 The "Stratis" apartment block – also called after a cloud formation – plays with the image of the stacked containers, which once dominated the docks. Dazzlingly white, like the yachts, which have meanwhile come to use the harbour, the apartment block also has its own gleaming moorings. For the gable end of the extended building the architects chose a sort of chequerboard pattern made of concrete elements and glass. The reliefs in the enclosed areas refer to the paintings of the artist Gordon Walters, who combined op art and traditional patterns in his works already in the 1960s – just as the architects today have succeeded in producing a subtle synthesis of contemporary building and Pacific traditions.

Q/R

Karim Rashid

Karim Rashid is a designer and lives in New York.
www.karimrashid.com

240–243 "Nooch Express is the quick food version of an established restaurant chain. Located in a mall in Singapore, the restaurant is a break from traditional fast food. Our challenge was to take a typically mundane or branded typography and interpret it from a more conceptual basis. We strove to create a space that was high energy, and reflected the speed of a "fast food" café. We used bright technical colours and strong curvilinear forms to emphasise speed. The cross section of the space is reflected on the facade of the restaurant. The window becomes the section; this space is merely part of a larger whole, cut at both ends like a log and capped for definition, again referencing the infinite extension of the fast food concept."

Casey Reas

Casey Reas is a designer and lives in Los Angeles.
www.reas.com

244–249 Casey Reas regards his works as choreographies, which engage the observer intellectually, emotionally and physically. Reas produces them with computer programmes specially designed for that purpose. This software arises from short sets of instructions in which the processes are described. Static images are only one

possible form, into which such instructions can be translated; others are language or machine code. Each of these forms makes it possible to regard the processes they describe from another perspective. Reas sees himself as a constructor of "machines with ways of behaving, which stimulate human perceptions and induce yearning. These ways of behaving arise in the interaction of individual and work."

David Reed

David Reed was born in San Diego, studied fine art at the Studio School in New York and has been living there ever since.

250/251 His works are meant as part of living and are not to be isolated in museums and galleries, David Reed declared in an interview. And he added: "Paintings belong where they are a part of everyday life and can be viewed in personal moments of daydreaming." In his painting, David Reed plays with clichéd images baroque in their styling. At the same time, he works in the tradition of abstract expressionism. The important thing is, however, that he adjusts his way of working to an image-making process, which seems to us run of the mill: film. As is clear from his colour handling, Reed paints in a vertical plane, just as if he was dealing with a succession of filmic scenes. The film itself is, as a strip, as a ribbon, a pictorial motif at the same time. And in addition, Reed uses colours corresponding to the Technicolor of film and he imparts the smooth, reflective surface of celluloid to his paintings. In this way, Reed weaves together elements of the decorative frieze, of cinematography and painting.

Gerhard Richter

Gerhard Richter is an artist and lives in Cologne.

Gerhard Richter once described his access to a world, which consists above all of photographic representations, with the formula "see everything, understand nothing". At the beginning of the 1960s, reproductions from magazines served him as exemplars, later he reached back to family photographs too. The mediated world became an archive for him, an "Atlas" of the pictures that he also exhibited on the occasion of the documenta X in Kassel. As if to preserve the remains of painting from disappearing, Richter invented a method, which allows the observer to identify, without any doubt, a pictorial motif as a photographic one, but at the same time to perceive the signs of the craft behind the painting process. His so-called blurs which remove from photography its dependability and with which chance, imperfection and dilettantism come into play, have in this way become his trademarks.

252/253 In his works "Silikat"(2003) and "Strontium" (2004), Richter has concerned himself with scientific processes of image reproduction, which make visible microstructures we cannot recognise with the naked eye. "Silikat" shows the enlargement of a tetrahedron structure, as this occurs in crystal lattices. Richter painted a dark circle with a Y symbol in the centre, which he repeats in twenty horizontal rows 350 times. The pictorial motif of "Strontium" is the molecular construction of alkaline-earth metal. The gigantic work consists of 130 C prints, which are printed with silicon onto acrylic panes. In the overview of the individual pieces, a pattern becomes visible, which is related to the principle of the Allover in painting. So the circle closes: as Richter began by imitating photography with the methods of painting, so, with the aid of photography, he now creates effects, which are well-known to us from painting.

Bridget Riley

Bridget Riley is an artist.
She lives in London and Vaucluse.

254/255 The British artist Bridget Riley works with repetition, perspectival reversal and counterpoint. For this reason, her pictures became in the 1960s the epitome of op art. She consistently distanced herself from this art movement, as she is actually concerned less with surprising visual effects than with plumbing rathermore various pictorial layers, which open up to her during the act of painting. From rigorous black and white works, she went over in 1967 to intensely contrastive organising of colour, as can be seen in "Chant 2". Riley came to the conclusion: "Colour energies need a virtually neutral vehicle if they are to develop uninhibitedly. The repeated stripe seems to meet these conditions." In 1992, Bridget Riley left structures of stripes behind and broadened her palette. Hence she used in producing "High Sky 2" twenty distinct single colours alongside black and white contrasts. The pictorial structure is based on a vertical register of wide bands, which is intersected by a collection of parallel diagonals. In the process of perceiving it, the picture seems to begin moving, the colour areas oscillate back and forward.

Rinzen

The Rinzen collective currently consists of five members who are working in Sydney, Brisbane and Berlin.
www.rinzen.com

256–261 For a calendar of the Japanese magazine "+81", the members of the Rinzen design-collective employed digital means to create a pattern with the appearance of a screen-print. Their Identity-Design for the exhibition "Paper and String" brings wrapping paper to mind, and for the Australian Record Industry Association music awards, they developed posters and invitation cards, which revolve around the subject of music notation. In their wallpaper for the Amsterdam branch of the advertising agency Wieden + Kennedy, they take up kitsch elements. Only on closer inspection does the observer notice that the detail is about death.

Peter Roehr

Peter Roehr was born in Lauenburg, Pomerania in 1944 and lived from 1955 to his death in 1968 in Frankfurt am Main.

262/263 "A picture has no point of existence, it happens everywhere. It could expand and keep going in all directions; it is in itself limitless, but then it would not be this one, but another picture. So: choosing of objects and deciding their quantity is the maker's only arbitrary work." What the artist Peter Roehr is here formulating in terms of his circa two hundred typo-montages, which he produced from 1963 with a typewriter on paper, that reveals an artistic programme. Peter Roehr thought that art, which wants to be of its times, has to be simple and cheap to produce. Above all, however, it should not testify to the signature of the artist but acknowledge its mechanical production.

S

Sadar Vuga Arhitekti

Sadar Vuga Arhitekti is a firm of architects that was founded in 1992 by Jurij Sadar and Bostjan Vuga in Ljubljana.
www.sadarvuga.com

264/265 Conspicuously projecting balconies, various openings for roof terraces and an irregular distribution of windows make the apartment block in Ljubljana (Slovenia) seem unusually shapely. In contrast, the pixel pattern of light blue and black ceramic panels has more of a flattened, graphical effect. The contradictory game with spatial perception becomes particularly obvious with the heavy black frames of the windows, which seem to lose themselves in the expanse.

Sauerbruch Hutton Architekten

Sauerbruch Hutton is a firm of architects founded in 1989 by Louisa Hutton and Matthias Sauerbruch. The firm runs offices in London and Berlin.
www.sauerbruchhutton.com

266/267 For the western facade of the glass high-rise, the architects chose vertical sunscreen panels in various red tones. Fixed between the double casings of the glass facade, they produce a complex rhythm of colour, which contrasts with the blue of the sky and the grey of the surroundings. According to the time of day and the direction of the light, the area of colour changes, as the panels can be individually adjusted by the staff.
The coloured blinds of the two technical buildings for the Photonics Centre in Berlin-Adlershof are reminiscent of light's colour spectrum and of the necessary darkening of laboratories. Interior-mounted sunscreen panels produce a flattened pattern, complemented by the correspondingly coloured supports for the facade's double casing.

268/269 Coloured glass panels envelop the seven-storey laboratory and office building as a reversible sunscreen and combine the different areas optically into a single construction.

270/271 The 115 metre long and 30 metre high warehouse gains its strong visual presence through the distribution of twenty different colours as small fragments. Broad tin panels, that are 25 cm high and 160 cm long, produce a complex pattern, the effect of which was previously tested in many studies and on a model.

Paul Simmons

The designer Paul Simmons founded his studio Timorous Beasties together with Alistair McAuley in 1990.
The firm designs and produces wallpapers, which are fabricated in a handcrafted screen-printing process or with modern computer technologies.
www.timorousbeasties.com

272–275 The wallpapers of designer Paul Simmons only appear conventional at first sight. His "Euro Damask" is reminiscent of baroque-inspired motifs, which repeat in the sequential pattern. Yet small "mistakes" disturb the symmetry and their formal indistinctness make the wallpaper reminiscent of a Rorschach test. Or it becomes a visual puzzle, as it is only the name of the wallpaper that indicates the European coastal formations, which serve as model for the pattern. Paul Simmon's patterns are contemporary interpretations of traditional motifs. Hence, "Glasgow Toile" is a somewhat macabre version of French models from the 18th century. On the traditional Toile-de-Jouy fabrics there were already, alongside rural idylls, motifs of farmers and workers as well, who are getting drunk and otherwise enjoying themselves. In the Glasgow version, the village marketplaces become high-rise scenes, complete with a supermarket. The women are courted no longer, but are already pushing prams. And a good-natured pipe-smoker becomes a junkie on a park bench. In this way, Paul Simmons serves up a remorseless, realistic description of his hometown.

Francis Soler

The architect Francis Soler founded his own firm of architects in Paris in 1985.
www.soler.fr

276–279 The Ministry of Culture and Communication, previously spread around many different locations in the city, was to be concentrated together in the centre of Paris. To that end, various buildings from different epochs were combined and added to. Nearby are the Palais Royal and the passage Vero-Dodat. A lattice of laser-cut stainless steel panels enveloped the heterogeneous ensemble and makes it hence appear a stand-alone. Six different motifs using vegetative lines generate in combination a pattern, which is at once modern and distantly reminiscent of motifs from art nouveau.

Rudolf Stingel

Rudolf Stingel, born in Murano, is an artist and lives in New York.

280–283 The installation "Home Depot" was to be seen in the Museum of Modern Art in Frankfurt am Main in 2004. A damask pattern covered walls, floor, pillar supports and part of the ceiling. That was provided by silver foil printed in red, which was fastened to Celotex panels. On one wall hung the painting "Roter Fisch" (Red Fish, 1992) by Sigmar Polke, on the opposite one a triptych by Rudolf Stingel, which repeated the damask pattern in the colours white on silver. If the walls and the floor were still unmarked at the opening, the space changed increasingly by dint of uncontrolled interventions: museum visitors were allowed to take away pieces of the screenprinted foil, so that the light brown surface of the Celotex panels gradually became visible. Underneath the beautiful appearance of the traditional system of décor, the supporting elements of the installation came into sight, which the artist had acquired in an American building supplies store with the name of "Home Depot".

Anisa Suthayalai

Anisa Suthayalai is a designer and lives in New York. She works for design agencies like 2x4 Studio and design:mw, among others.
www.bydefault.org

284–287 For Vitra, Anisa Suthayalai created ornaments, which are reminiscent of mandalas and which reflect the furniture manufacturer's product lines. "Vitra is a successful European furniture company, but for the American market it can seem cold and inaccessible. So we beautified it and made it more friendly. We reintroduced Vitra in an approachable way using a more recognizable language: Furniture blossoms like beautiful flowers." says a statement by Anisa Suthayalai.

T

Philip Taaffe

Philip Taaffe is an artist and lives in New York.

288–291 Since the 1980s Philip Taaffe has been looking for ways and means to make the ornamental into a pictorial theme again. He orientates himself after Islamic miniatures, which foretell the recreation of paradise on earth; he finds his motifs in southern Italy, but readily borrows from William Morris's pattern books as well. Hence his interaction with painting is closely linked to a questioning of the basis by which artists from Europe and the United States have long been used to absorbing foreign cultures.

Rosemarie Trockel

Rosemarie Trockel is an artist and lives in Cologne.

292/293 The legend "Made in Germany" is woven at regular intervals into the material bearing it. Rosemarie Trockel inserts such logos, familiar from commerce and politics, repeatedly into her works in wool. These knitted pictures are not, for instance, the product of women's handiwork, but they are produced by a computer controlled machine according to the artist's instructions. In this way, Rosemarie Trockel achieves a reversal of value-systems: on the one hand, the techniques of industrial mass production are extended ad absurdum, as the artist uses them to produce a unique piece. On the other hand, the logo loses its effect in the context of a serial Allover. It can no longer signal something particularly valuable. And in addition, Rosemarie Trockel's knitted pictures are permeated by references specific to art. "Freude" (Joy) refers to Sigmar Polke's picture "Carl Andre in Delft", an ironic commentary on minimal art.

Jochen Twelker

Jochen Twelker is an artist and lives in Berlin.
www.jochentwelker.de

294–299 "Is it a flag or is it a painting?" The red, white and blue stars and stripes, which the American artist Jasper Johns applied to the canvas in encaustic-technique in the 1950s, triggered an art-philosophical debate on the complicated relationship of model and depiction, of image and object, which still has not been concluded. It was particularly vexing that it was impossible to decide whether the painted flag was an abstract or a representational image. Jochen Twelker's images demonstrate that posing this question can have its rewards even today. What at first seems like a cautiously arranged collection of stripes, squares and floral patters, reveals itself on closer inspection as the partially enlarged depiction of a group of people who are all wearing patterned t-shirts and shirts. Or as a tunnel vision into a wardrobe. Or as a surprise meeting with a cheap goods table, on which the most diverse kinds of material abound. Or as a view of praying muslims, who have donned soccer jerseys. Jochen Twelker makes possible the impossible: his style of painting has flat fields and contours, is abstract and representational, popular and self-reflexive, serious and humourous, all at the same time.

U/V

Victor Vasarely

Victor Vasarely was a painter and a graphic artist. He was born in Péco in 1906 and moved to Paris in 1930.
From 1961 on, he lived in Annet-sur-Marne.
In 1997, the Foundation Vasarely was opened in Aix-en-Provence.
Victor Vasarely died in Paris in 1997.

300/301 Setting out from the conviction that what is uncontrolled and irrational in art has to be overcome, Victor Vasarely executed a series of drawings with zebras as its motif at the end of the 1930s. Dealing with a pattern, which appears in nature, was the foundation for Vasarely's later op art pictures. Vasarely succeeded in achieving 3-D effects across a picture's spread without using centralised perspective. To do this, he used compression, distortion and the bending of parallel lines and squares as well as moiré effects. Vasarely's goal was to democratise art in the form of freely reproducible multiples. From the 1960s on, he acted more as an author of ideas and left the execution to assistants.

W

Marcel Wanders

Marcel Wanders is a designer and lives in Amsterdam.
www.marcelwanders.com

302–305 With his objects, Marcel Wanders steps right into the middle of the discourse about ornamentation and function. His "Crochet Table" could well be an example of the only crocheted table in the history of design. To decorate it with a lace cloth would be completely pointless. In the same way, Wanders joins decorative and constructive elements together in his "Flower Chair": by combining numerous blossoms fashioned from steel into a gleaming, silver seat, he sublimates the basic shape of the lattice.
He also works on the deconstruction of patterns with his glass-mosaic objects, which he has created for Bisazza: the facade of a sauna room illustrates with its enlarged pixel-ornamentation the relationship of digital aesthetic to time-honoured mosaic techniques – on the faces of the steps, the pattern disintegrates as in an extreme zoom in on a computer graphic. In a bathroom, the enlarged ornamentation moreover extends behind the washbasin in sheets, as if it wanted to comment on the collection of styles it carries.

Heinrich Weid

Heinrich Weid is an artist.
He lives in Baruth near Berlin.

Heinrich Weid self-confidently treads the narrow boundary that divides fine and applied art. He has created numerous art-in-building projects and developed a wall-design, which transforms the car as status symbol, into a pattern from silver foil for the publishers' premises of the "Donaukurier" in Ingolstadt. For each project, Heinrich Weid concentrates on one motif, which he interrogates as to its present-day function and meaning aided by the principle of repetition and mirror-imaging.

306/307 Heinrich Weid prescribed the motif of the shell, which is not only a company logo but also a symbol of the pilgrims and of erotic love, for the urban space of Düsseldorf. The pavilion he constructed by using the motif of the shell does not invite you to stay. Benches are missing and this temporary architecture offers no roof over your head. In this way, the pavilion becomes a sign of what has gone missing in cities: open spaces, tranquil areas and places where people can meet.

308/309 For Siemens AG in Munich, Heinrich Weid constructed a pavilion, which can be viewed as a sculpture and used as a piece of architecture. Pushing a button activates an electric motor, by which the pavilion revolves on its eight wheels around itself. In addition, the artist uses the glistening silver surface of stainless steel, zinc and aluminium for a play on words, which turns on the relationship between the sexes: the name of the patron becomes SIE (she) and MEN. Munich's revolving pavilion stands, round and ornamental, across from the practical configuration of the facade of the Siemens AG branch offices.

310/311 Imitating wooden surfaces with imprinting and painting has long been tradition. The possibility of copying wood in ceramics also fascinated Heinrich Weid. And so he developed a stoneware dinner service in 2003, which cites its models and simultaneously ironises them in the way it is painted. In a multi-stage process, moulds were taken first, then objects were fired in an electric oven, glazed and finally decorated. The raised knotholes received their structure via adhesive images, which were created through the screenprinting transfer process. The service's plates, mugs, cake stands, sauce boats and cutlery find completion as a comprehensive work of art with "wooden" accessories like a table cloth, chairs, a lamp and wallpaper.

Hanna Werning

Hanna Werning is a graphic designer and lives in Stockholm.
www.byhanna.com

312–315 Together with her colleague Joakim Ericson, the Swedish designer Hanna Werning has constructed from found objects a machine, which utilises a permanent marker to apply random, but regular patterns on white rolls of wallpaper. Regarding her series "Animal Flowers", she talks about wallpaper-posters. The prints can be hung on the wall like posters, are capable of connecting on all sides and only in combination with each other reveal that they are the parts of a meta-pattern.

X/Y

Ekrem Yalçindağ

Ekrem Yalçindağ was born in Gölbasi, Turkey.
He studied fine art in Izmir and at the Städelschule in Frankfurt am Main.
Ekrem Yalçindağ lives in Frankfurt am Main.

316/317 Ekrem Yalçindağ's pictures come about in the course of a multi-stage, time-consuming process: he begins by structuring the canvas with the aid of pencil lines drawn freehand. In doing that, he produces variations of about thirty different blossom shapes, without using templates. In a second procedure, he paints over the fine pencil lines with silver. Then, with a whisper-thin brush he paints in, stroke for stroke, the empty spaces between the dividing lines precise to the millimetre. This process of applying colour often stretches over several months. It is repeated often enough for the colour to become palpably raised and the surface of the picture transforms itself into a relief.

Douglas Young

Born in Hong Kong, the designer Douglas Young trained as an architect at Sheffield University and the Architectural Association in London.
In 1996, he founded the design office G.O.D. together with his partner Benjamin Lau.
www.god.com.hk

318/319 The majority of the merchandise of the design office G.O.D. based in Hong Kong is self-branded by a multi-disciplinary design team led by Douglas Young. The Chinese metropolis Hong Kong belongs among the most densely populated places in the world. As a result of social and finally architectural changes in China today in many of the huge apartment blocks of the poorer quarters, every tenant fixes their own, unmistakable letterbox at the entrance. To enlarge their living space, many residents build metal structures onto their windows or balconies besides. In both cases, Douglas Young has adapted the visual results of these living conditions into patch-work-like patterns.

Z

Peter Zimmermann

The artist Peter Zimmermann studied at the Academy of Fine Arts in Stuttgart.
He lives in Cologne.

320–323 In the 1980s, German artist Peter Zimmermann caused a sensation by making paintings of book titles. and in addition, his new pictures have their origin in existing images, which he modifies with a computer programme. The models can be enlarged until they lose focus and betray their matrices in that process. Peter Zimmermann translates the motifs he discovers from computer modification of his images into painting as he pours synthetic resin onto canvas. The patterns that have digital transformation to thank for their structure, display surprisingly extensive similarities to pictorial developments in painting from the 1950s: informal and abstract expressionism. In a paradoxical twist, Peter Zimmermann unites in this way traditional and technologically innovative image-making processes.

About the editors

Petra Schmidt is editor-in-chief of form – The European Design Magazine. She lives in Frankfurt/Main. **Annette Tietenberg** is an art historian, critic and curator. Currently, she is Visiting Professor of Art, Architecture and Design at Burg Giebichenstein in Halle (Saale). She lives in Heppenheim on the Hessian Bergstraße. **Ralf Wollheim** is a critic of architecture and an exhibition organiser. He lives in Berlin.

Acknowledgements

We owe special thanks to the artists, designers and architects involved. We are also grateful to all the photographers, who generously made their images available to us. Furthermore, we wish to thank all the museums, art associations and galleries, which assisted us in our search for image material.

We would like to thank all those whose commitment enabled this book to be realised: **Monika Anderson** Cologne, **Reinder Bakker** Rotterdam, **Meike Behm** Frankfurt/Main, **Ulrike Bernhard** Berlin, **Peter Blythe** Toronto, **Joachim Boepple** Berlin, **Ute Bongartz** Cologne, **Daniel Bosshard** Zurich, **Lionel Bovier** Geneva, **Jenny Brown** Tokyo, **Patrick Coan** Stockholm, **Richard Collins** Berlin, **Gianni Degryse** Ghent, **Silja van der Does** Darmstadt, **AA Bronson** New York, **Mirko Driller** Berlin, **Konstanze Ell** Cologne, **Molly Epstein** New York, **Matthias Frings** Berlin, **Barbara Galleri** Milan, **Lucy Gauntlett** Auckland, **Siegfried K. Geyer** Heidenheim, **Markus Gomon** Leipzig, **Karola Grässlin** Brunswick, **Karin Grausam** Vienna, **Susan Grinols** San Francisco, **Dr. Lucius Grisebach** Nuremberg, **Marcus Gründel** Brunswick, **Thomas Hauser** Bern, **Volker Heinen** Berlin, **Dr. Thomas Heyden** Nuremberg, **Andreas Hild** München, **Dr. René Hirner** Heidenheim, **Anneke Holz** Berlin, **Danella Hocevar** Toronto, **Michael Janssen** Cologne, **Dr. Stan Jones** Hamilton (NZ), **Desiree de Jong** Breda, **Frans de Jong** Rotterdam, **Eileen Kästner** Neu-Isenburg, **Cecilia Karlsson** London, **Nozomi Kawagishi** Tokyo, **Alina Klemm** Brunswick, **Sabine Klemm** Leipzig, **Christine Knies** Neu-Isenburg, **Florian Koch** Frankfurt/Main, **Jane Koh** New York, **Olga Korstanje** Rotterdam, **Dr. Mario Kramer** Frankfurt/Main, **Charlotte Kruk** Paris, **Friedrich Loock** Berlin, **Peter Lütje** Frankfurt/Main, **Dwight Marica** Rotterdam, **Jon Mason** New York, **Kai Middendorff** Frankfurt/Main, **Sarah Miltenberger** Berlin, **Birgit Müller** Cologne, **Werner Müller** Berlin, **Janine Murphy** New York, **Hideyuki Nakayama** Tokyo, **Alice Panzer** Birsfelden, **Jessica M. Pearson** New York, **Michael Rock** New York, **Andy Ryan** Cambridge, **Maresa Rohrer** New York, **Gudrun Sack** Berlin, **Syma Sayyahs** Teheran, **Katrin Schal** Rotterdam, **Stephanie Schleiffer** Zurich, **Marcel Schmid** Zurich, **Dr. Ulrich Schmidt** Basel, **Barbara Schroeder** New York, **Thomas Schröder** Frankfurt/Main, **Martin Siegmund** Berlin, **Bernd Slutzky** Frankfurt/Main, **Dr. Heliod Spiekermann** Haan, **Birgit Suk** Nuremberg, **Gerrit Terstiege** Frankfurt/Main, **Sarah Thompson** New York, **Tal Trost** Zurich, **Maike Truschkowski** Frankfurt/Main, **Katrin Tüffers** Frankfurt/Main, **Miki Uono** Tokyo, **Michèle C. Vasarely** Chicago, **Dorothea Wagner** Basel, **Thomas Wagner** Heppenheim, **Markus Weisbeck** Frankfurt/Main, **Anja Welle** Hamilton (NZ), **Christina Werner** Berlin, **Dr. Katrin Wiethege** Bregenz, **Femke de Wild** Amsterdam, **Christine Wong** Hong Kong, **Haegue Yang** Berlin, **Maki Yamaji** Surry Hills, **Olga Zhuravleva** Amsterdam

Photo Credits

Bettina Allamoda 22/23
Haleh Anvari 34/35
Coco Amardeil 174, 177
Artothek Kunstfotoarchiv Weilheim 236/237
Claus Bach 20/21
Bantam 110
Hélène Binet 62/63
Studio Jurgen Bey 54/55
Jan Bitter 266–271
Studio Tord Boontje 58/59, 60
Nicola Borel 276–279
Stefan Bressel 68–71
Stefanie Bürkle 76–81
Museum Boijmans van Beuningen, Rotterdam 104/105
Caratsch de Pury & Luxembourg, Zürich 36–39
Claudia Caviezel 82/83
Federico Cedrone 304
Benny Chan 198
Roderick Coyne 26 (below left)
Gordon R. Christmas 191
Peter Clarke 166
Richard Davies 102/103
Colin Davison 202/203
Alan Dimmick 272–275
Julian Dodd 175, 176

Aaron Diskin 95
Alberto Ferrero 222–225
Georges Fessey 220/221
Sascha Fuis 290/291
Jürgen Gebhardt 156–159
Luftbild Geyer 216/217
Michael Heinrich 128–131
Silke Helmerding 294–299
Andrew Hobbs 167
Eduard Hueber/archphoto 42/43
Bill Jacobson 190
Michael Janssen Galerie, Köln 320–323
Richard Johnson 24/25
Katsuhisa Kida Photography 152/153
Silvia Knüppel & Damien Regamey 154/155
Annette Kradisch 255, 292
Foto Krust & Peters 46–49
Achim Kukulies 192–197, 293
Kunstverein Braunschweig 162/163, 164/165
Alan Lai 26 (above and below right)
Rüdiger Lainer 170–173
Michael Lin 182–187
Jochen Littkemann 230–235
Margit Lukács 72–75
Bruce Mau Inc. 199–201
Johannes Marburg 208/209
Ignacio Martinez 188/189

Trevor Mein 140/141, 168/169
Kai Middendorff 316/317
Muga Miyahara 204/205, 207
Moroso 56/57, 61
Nacasa & Partners 136–139
Carsten Nicolai 210–213
Kurt Paulus 254
Alessandro Perdini 57, 61
Goran Potkonjak 250/251
Tom Powel 92–94
Karim Rashid Inc. 240–243
Dusan Reljin 50/51, 52/53
Patrick Reynolds 238/239
Ricordi & Sfera 90/91
Christian Richters 27, 96/97, 178/179
Christian Röder 44/45
Friedrich Rosenstiel 252
Philippe Ruault (O.M.A.) 226–229
Andy Ryan 132–135
Fine Arts Museum of San Francisco 253
Marcel Schmid 180/181
Uwe Schmidt 112/113
Axel Schneider 262–263, 280–283
Lothar Schnepf 28–33
Bernd Sinterhauf 120–125
Steve Sloman 288/289
Margherita Spiluttini 126/127

Daniel Sumesgutner 148–151
Hisao Suzuki 264–265
Markus Tretter 160/161
Ottavio Tomasini 305
Michèle C. Vasarely 300–301
Marcel Wanders 302/303
Uwe Walter 214–215
Heinrich Weid 306–311
Hanna Werning/Joakim Ericson 312–313
Bruno Weiß 114/115
Makoto Yoshida 40/41
Douglas Young 318/319
Jens Ziehe 18/19
2x4 Studio 284–287
Zwinger Galerie, Berlin 118/119

Imprint
Petra Schmidt, Annette Tietenberg, Ralf Wollheim (eds.)
Patterns in Design, Art and Architecture

Editors: Meike Behm, Ralf Wollheim
Editorial Contributor: Mirko Driller
Translations: Stan Jones, Anja Welle
Graphics: Surface Gesellschaft für Gestaltung mbH
Maike Truschkowski, Katrin Tüffers, Markus Weisbeck
Production: Medien Profis GmbH, Leipzig

This book is also available in a German language edition.
(ISBN 3-7643-7749-6)

A CIP catalogue record for this book is available from the Library of Congress,
Washington D.C., USA.

Bibliographic information provided by Die Deutsche Bibliothek:
Die Deutsche Bibliothek lists this publication in the Deutsche Nationalbibliografie;
detailed bibliographic data is available on the internet at http://dnb.ddb.de.

© 2007 Birkhäuser – Publishers for Architecture
P.O. Box 133, CH-4010 Basel, Switzerland
Part of Springer Science+Business Media

© 2007 for the reproduced works vested in their originators and their legal successors.
© 2007 ProLitteris, Zurich for the reproduced works by Bettina Allamoda, Birgit Antoni, Stefanie Bürkle,
Silvia Knüppel & Damien Regamey, Thomas Mass, Carsten Nicolai, Olaf Nicolai, Susanne Paesler,
Peter Roehr, Rosemarie Trockel, Jochen Twelker, Victor Vasarely, Peter Zimmermann

We have taken pains to locate all copyright holders. Should we have not been successful in
individual cases, copyright claims should be addressed to the publishers.

Printed on acid-free paper produced from chlorine-free pulp. TCF ∞
Printed in Germany

ISBN-10: 3-7643-7750-X
ISBN-13: 978-3-7643-7750-2

9 8 7 6 5 4 3 2 1
http://www.birkhauser.ch